TO: LEAH

Quinn, the Rottweiler

A Story of a Dog Dealing with Cancer

Maryly Turner

iUniverse, Inc.
New York   Bloomington

Quinn, the Rottweiler
A Story of a Dog Dealing with Cancer

iUniverse books may be ordered through booksellers or by contacting:

iUniverse
1663 Liberty Drive
Bloomington, IN 47403
www.iuniverse.com
1-800-Authors (1-800-288-4677)

Because of the dynamic nature of the Internet, any Web addresses or links contained in this book may have changed since publication and may no longer be valid. The views expressed in this work are solely those of the author and do not necessarily reflect the views of the publisher, and the publisher hereby disclaims any responsibility for them.

ISBN: 978-1-4401-7493-3 (sc)
ISBN: 978-1-4401-7491-9 (dj)
ISBN: 978-1-4401-7492-6 (ebk)

Printed in the United States of America

iUniverse rev. date: 11/16/2009

Contents

ACKNOWLEDGMENTS

Originally, I wanted to share Quinn's story with kids 13 to 16 years old, who were going through chemo treatments. So I called my friend, Josh Gernert, to see if he would like to read my manuscript and give me his thoughts. At the age of 19 months he was diagnosed with leukemia. He is now a 14 year old healthy survivor who would be just the one that I was looking for. Not only did he read it, he turned in a book report, receiving an A.

A huge thanks to Kathy Shearn, long-time dog-lover friend, who when I told her I was writing Quinn's story, freely offered to edit. Our friendship started 20 years ago on a morning when I was at a baseball field, putting my first Rottweiler, Morton, through obedience lessons. She was walking her two dogs, and she stopped to watch and asked questions about training. Over the years she has put in countless hours volunteering at the local animal shelter. That too, deserves a big thank you.

To my long-time friend, Janis Cox, who loves and has rescued many unwanted dogs in need of a "forever home," where they end up the lucky ones, getting to wrap Janis around their paws.

A big thanks to Sandy Hoyt, who has the same passion for Rottweilers as I do. Thank you for all of our endless doggie conversations and the wonderful help you and your husband, Ray, give to the many dog owners in this community.

To Cindy Hoyle, who loved and enjoyed Quinn's story, learning that you can have conversations with your dogs, besides just calling them to eat.

A thanks to Pat Elliott, a former classmate and long-time friend, for reading Quinn's story and sending a note back saying, "didn't know your dogs had such a great home with you---lucky!!" And to Pat's daughter, Erin Huizenga, who is Annie's mom, for giving me her input and letting Annie be a part of my dog family. We love Annie as did Quinn. Because of the story, Erin now gives Annie Frostie Paws, the ice cream for dogs.

To Ginger's mom, Becky Rupe, who rescued Ginger on doomsday from the animal shelter, and gave her a loving home.

A special thanks to Dr. Sara Rice, VMD; without her the book would not have happened. She asked me one day how the book was coming along, after I had opened my big mouth, saying I was going to write about Quinn and his cancer, and I hadn't even started it. I cannot thank Sara enough for all the care and devotion she gave Quinn during the battle to save his life. Her positive attitude helped me so much during those tiring months of chemo treatments. You are the best.

To Drs. Sommers, LaRue, Burns, for your care throughout the months treating Quinn. I thank you all from the bottom of my heart. And Dr. Bennett, (the new/young one,) who was there to send Quinn on his journey to the Rainbow Bridge, bless you. You are on your way to becoming a wonderful veterinarian. You handled a most difficult task in the short time since you started practicing veterinary care. I thank you.

To the staff at Mendocino Animal Hospital: Denise, Terry, Gina, Kathy, Michelle, Tina, Michael, and last but not least, Quinn's buddy, Danny. The love you showed and gave to Quinn is why I bring my pets to MAH. I thank you all for helping Quinn learn how to be a good boy at the clinic.

The girls on the front desk, who so freely gave out treats to Quinn, thank you. Jane, Susan, Michelle, Erin, and April. You made our weekly and bi-weekly visits better. Quinn loved you all.

To my family and my daughter, Bobbie Persico, who told me to get off my butt and start writing. She knows what a procrastinator I am.

I hope that by reading Quinn's story, one will learn that the extra hug or pat on your dog's head will mean so much to these wonderful companions. They have too short a time with us. Love and enjoy every minute with them.

CHAPTER 1

A New Beginning

It's just another lonely night as I walk slowly into the cold, wet shed. I'm getting ready to bed down for one of the last chilly, miserable nights here, not yet knowing that my life is about to change, leaving this all behind. I say chilly and miserable because I'm out here in this shed alone, and my papa and his family are inside the main house. Two little dogs also live inside. They have no idea what it's like to sleep out in this shed. My papa loves me, but he thinks because I'm a big dog that I'm okay out here. Oh how I'd love to sleep inside like the little dogs do.

The sun is finally coming up the next morning, and I am laying on the cement walkway, waiting for the ground to thaw out from the sun warming the yard. There is a guide-line that goes from the shop to the back-porch. I have on a leather collar, which is connected to a chain. I don't like my collar because it rubs away the fur on my neck. This chain slides back and forth on the guideline, letting me jump around and trot over to my papa where he sits on his chair by the kitchen door. I hear the telephone ring. After the girl hangs up, I hear her saying that a lady is interested in coming to meet the dog in the ad. The ad reads, 'ADULT MALE ROTTWEILER-FREE TO A GOOD HOME' I wonder, would that be about me? I'm a grown Rottweiler who will turn eight years old in a couple of days. I'm laying here soaking up the sun, wondering and worrying if I've done something bad, when I hear the girl tell my papa that it's for the best; Papa is getting older and can't get around as well as when I first came here to live with him and his family.

Before I go any further with my story, let me introduce myself. My name is Chong. They joke about how I had a littermate named Cheech. I don't understand, but for some reason everybody laughs when they hear my name, thinking it's a funny joke. They don't know that it hurts when I hear them laughing at me. Don't people know that dogs have feelings? Sometimes it can be very damaging, enough to break a good dog down, and trust will be lost. Some dogs have jobs they are expected to perform, while others are pets and just want to make their people happy. I know that's what I'm here to do.

I am hungry, even though my food dish is full. I don't like the way it tastes. I take a bite and try not to think about how awful it is. In keeping my bowl filled, my family thinks I have plenty to eat. As always, I end up eating or go without. They mean well and think that everything is okay. I have no idea that there are better ways for a dog to be treated.

The lady that phoned wants to come and meet me. The girl tells her that today is not a good day to see me. They think I've got a sticker or a thorn in my foot. My left front leg hurts me so bad; sometimes I have trouble standing or walking on it. Because of this, my family has to take me to see my veterinarian. Going to the vet is fun, because that's usually the only time I get to go for a ride. Riding in the car is my very favorite thing to do. It's been a long time since I saw my veterinarian, so the car rides don't happen very often. My vet checks me over and tells the girl that I have something called arthritis. He gives her pain medication for me to take. A couple of days go by and I'm feeling a little bit better.

My papa is sitting on his chair on the back-porch. I like to sit in front of him and offer my paw. When he doesn't shake it, I offer my other paw. I try to please him by shaking hands. He likes that as much as I do. My papa used to throw the ball for me. Come to think about it, I don't know what happened to that ball. Maybe my papa can't play anymore. Playing ball is my second favorite thing to do, after riding in the car.

I'm taking a nap, dreaming about chasing the ball, when I hear the sound of a car coming up the road to my house. I wonder, who could it be? I jump up and stretch really tall. I see two ladies getting out of a van; they are talking to the girl and my papa. One of the ladies gives me a cookie, and I notice that she has more cookies in her hand. I'm being the best boy I can be. Everybody is smiling. I have a happy smile on my face, and my stubby tail will not stop wagging. I am a happy boy. I like the lady, but she leaves. I wish she would've stayed longer, because she seemed to like me. Maybe if she stayed, we could've played ball. It's been so long since anybody played with me. My family is telling me that she will be back tomorrow to take me home with her. I'm going to live in a family with two other dogs and even a cat! I've heard about cats, but they never come close enough for me to get to know.

I go to sleep in the shed, and dream about my new family. What will they be like? Will I be on a chain? Where will I sleep? I'm in the middle of a good snooze, when I awake to the sound of a car coming up the road to my papa's house. I come outside to see the lady that was here yesterday. The girl and papa are talking to her. She is holding a leather leash in her hand. Everybody is smiling and nodding, as the girl undoes my chain. The lady fastens the leash to my collar and walks me out to the car. Oh boy, it looks like I get to go for a ride with her. I am so excited about that! There's lots of room in back for me to lay down, as the seats are flatten out. The lady turns to me, telling me that I'm a good boy.

She says that we will be at my new home very soon. Off we go down the bumpy dirt road, followed by a rolling mass of dust billowing up behind us. I love riding in the car. It won't be long before we reach town, as we are on the freeway now and going a lot faster.

When we get to my new house, the lady gets out and opens the gate. She parks the car and lets me out. I sniff around the carport, smelling the other dogs' scents. I trot up onto the porch and see two dogs in a kennel. They are as anxious to meet me as I am to meet them. The one who catches my eye first is the little red dog, a Terrier/hound mix, with a white chest, sox, and a white tip on his tail. Because of time, his face is now dusted with a powdered chalky-white colored mask that goes to the top of his eyebrows. He is about half my size. They call him Ernie and he is eleven years old. The second dog is a black, Border Collie/lab mix. She is very pretty, with a shiny black coat, a white chest, sox, and white tip on her tail, like Ernie. She is almost as big as me. What's not good about this is she weighs about the same as I do, and I'm a male

Rottweiler, who should weigh a lot more than she does. Her name is Rosey, and she's four years old.

The lady lets the dogs out of their kennel. We meet and start to play and run all around the yard, jumping and chasing each other as we begin our friendship. I like them and they like me too. They tell me that it's almost dinnertime, and I'm put in the kennel by myself. The lady explains, it's because Ernie and Rosey eat their dinner very fast, and since I'm new here, they will try to eat my dinner also! She goes to feed them while I wait for her to bring me mine. The door opens and she puts my dish down. This food smells so very good, and a lot better than my old food! Yummm! It even has some broth in it. Slowly, I eat my dinner. When the lady sees that I'm done, she opens the gate. Rosey and Ernie rush in and start licking my dish.

We run around the yard and play tag. Oh, I'm having the time of my life with my new family. I sure would like to meet the cat, but I haven't seen her yet. Ernie tells me that she has been up on the rooftop watching me. He said that she was jumped by another Rottweiler and had her jaw broken. I tell Ernie, "I would never hurt her, she is part of my new family."

It's getting colder now that it's later in the day, and the sun is going down on one of the best days I've had in a long, long time. I'm not sure where I'll be sleeping. I remember seeing a doghouse in the kennel and wonder, if that's where I'll be. Where do the other dogs sleep? It's now dark outside and the lady opens the door to let us in. Ernie and Rosey race right by me, but I'm not sure if I'm supposed to come inside along with them. But the lady calls me too, she has cookies for us! WOW! We get cookies at night!?

It's so nice being in the house I really don't like the cold, and my leg seems to ache more than when it's warm. Soon it's time to go to bed. Will I have to go sleep in that doghouse outside? I follow the other two dogs and the lady down the stairs to a small room where there is a nice big stove in the corner. A fire is burning, making the room warm and cozy. Rosey and Ernie automatically go to their beds and curl up. The lady shows me a big flannel blanket that is folded into a square on the floor near the stove.

"This is your bed, Chong," she says, pointing to the blanket.

I can't believe this is where I get to sleep! This is something I had no idea big dogs got to do. It's like being in a dream. All I remember was an old throw rug or the thin worn out blanket with a couple of holes in it. And when it was rainy and cold, the blanket was damp. When I was a younger guy before my shoulder and leg started bothering me, the weather didn't make any difference to me. I really never paid to much attention to how cold it was, as long as I got to be in the shed at night, and out of the rain. When it started to get warmer, I would usually just stretch out on the cement walkway and fall asleep there. That way, I could keep one of my ears cocked for any unusual sounds in the night. I've never slept inside of a house, or next to a warm stove before. The lights go out, and everyone is bedded down for the night. I dream about the car ride, my new family, and if my papa is okay. I miss him and wonder if he misses me too.

It's now morning and the lady lets us out to take care of what dogs do first thing in the morning. She calls us back in for our cookies. Not only do we get cookies at night, but in the morning too! This is something that never happened at my old house. Maybe I got a cookie or two if and when someone thought about it. But never in the morning and at night.

Ernie and Rosey are called to the front door and let outside. The lady then walks back to the kitchen where she is fixing breakfast for me. She sets my bowl down on a plastic bucket that is turned upside down, so it is higher up off the floor. With the bowl up higher I notice that my shoulder doesn't hurt as much. Looking in the bowl I see some lumpy white stuff mixed in with the kibble. It smells really delicious, but I have no idea what it is. She says to me, "Chong you are going to love this, it's called cottage cheese." I also can smell chicken broth in there. I eat slowly and every bite or two, I stop to look at the lady, thinking to myself how nice she is to me. Finally I'm finished, when she goes to open the door to let the other two dogs back in. Ernie races ahead of Rosey to my bowl and starts licking a couple of pieces of kibble that are left. While he is busy licking the bowl clean, Rosey sniffs around the base of the bucket and gobbles down the ones that had hit the floor.

The phone rings, and I follow the lady over as she picks it up to answer it. I sit in front of her listening to what she is saying. It sounds like she's telling someone about me.

"Yes I got the dog. The one that your mother went with me to see. His name is Chong, but somehow I don't feel it quite fits him. Chong sounds funny, so I'm going to change it," she laughs as she winks at me. She hangs up the phone and gives me a loving scratch on my head.

"Chong, this weekend you're going to meet my oldest granddaughter. You're going to love her. Her name is Ashley."

As soon as Rosey heard that, she ran inside. "Ashley! Ashley's coming? Did I hear that right?" she asked with excitement, "Ernie, Ashley's coming!"

I look at her and ask, "Who's Ashley?"

"Only my best friend who loves to take me down to the field and throw the ball farther than mom can. She is so much fun.

"She might take us on a walk!" she informs me.

"Really? I love walks. Would she take me too?"

"I don't know, but she'll take me for sure."

Ernie butts in, "And she gives us cookies all the time."

"But don't make her angry. She's firmer than our mom," Rosey adds looking at the lady, "She'll make you do what she says."

"Don't forget about the cookies afterwards," Ernie says jumping up and down, turning all around at the same time. Boy that guy loves cookies. He is always sniffing around the kitchen floor, hoping he will find some crumbs. The lady says that Ashley will be here in a few days and that she loves dogs as much as the lady does. Since I love kids so much I want to meet her. A few days pass and we are all put in the kennel along with being told. "Be good, I'm going to go get Ashley."

Rosey starts getting excited hearing that, wagging her tail back and forth; thumping it against the kennel gate. Time passes by and soon I hear the car pull in. The lady and a girl come up on to the porch. They both look down.

"There he is! Look at that face! And doesn't he kind look like old Mortie to you?" The lady asks the girl, who I assume must be Ashley.

"Yeah, kind of. He's the same type as Mort. Not the blocky, square looking Rottweiler that you see at dog shows."

"Ernie, Ernie, Ashley's here! Ashley's here!" shouts Rosey.

"Yep, I see her Rose, that's her" Ernie answers back with a silly smirk on his face.

They go into the house and soon I hear the lady coming down the stairs to let us inside. She opens the door and Rosey jumps and pushes past her, flying up the stairs. Banging the door against the wall. Slam! Bang!

"Ashley!" I hear her shouting in excitement.

"Rosey, Rosey! How's my girl?"

We make our way up the stairs and I can see her up close. She smiles at me and greets Ernie.

"Ernesto! How's the little man?" Ernie wags his tail as she scratches his back.

She then turns to me and kneels down,

"Hey Chong," She says softly offering out her hand to me.

I walk over to her and sniff all around her. She smells of other dogs and a cat. She softly pets my head as I sit down and offer her my paw. I like her right away, because not only does she like to shake hands, she comes across as a dog lover, just like the lady said. I hear the lady tell about my appointment tomorrow with my new veterinarian, Dr. Rice. When I hear this I wonder if I'll like her or not, and what she's like.

As the lady and Ashley sit and talk inside, I follow my new friends out to the yard to play. This is when they show me a gap in the fence, where we can talk to the big wolf-like dog next door. His name is Dakota, and he is staring back at us through the opening in the ivy. He lunges at the fence making it shake back and forth. The ivy is keeping the fence up, as it is entwined through the boards. It seems like he could rip the fence down if he wanted. Ernie is getting all excited, as he is up on his hind legs, jumping at the gap in the fence. He is making Dakota very irritated.

"Why do you want to tease him like that?" I ask.

"Cause it makes him mad," Ernie laughs, "And he can't get me!"

"Gee, I thought you were going to introduce me to a new friend?" No wonder Dakota's got an attitude, with all the teasing going on. I hear his mom calling him away from the fence. At the same time, the lady comes out and shouts at us, "That's enough!"

Ernie and Rosey turn away from the fence and race up the stairs leading to the porch. I am being called, "Chong, come!", She yells at me.

I sure don't like the way my name sounds, and I hope Dakota doesn't hear it. I'm running up the stairs, following the other two into the house. Where...she gives each of us another cookie!

After we eat our cookies, Ashley and Rosey are standing at the door. In Ashley's hand are a leather leash and a ball. "Granny, I'm taking Rosey for a walk down to the field. Be back in a while."

Ernie runs up with them to the gate whining on how he doesn't get to go. "That's not fair! I wanna' go! Why don't I get to go?" he sniffles.

I trot up there to see what is going on, wondering if I'll be able to go too. "Hey, I'll take you guys next. Okay!", Ashley tells us.

She smiles at Ernie and me. I trot back down the driveway and through the carport with, Ernie following me. The lady is standing there watching us. Just as we get to the porch, the phone rings. It's Tina from the animal hospital reminding us about tomorrow's appointment. Turning to me she says. "Tomorrow you get to meet Dr. Rice."

We go back out to the porch, where the lady combs through my coat, removing the dead hair, making me glossy black in the sun light.

Ernie and I hear the sound of the gate unlocking as Ashley and Rosey return. We take off running up the driveway to meet them. Ernie is very excited asking Rosey about all the things that they did down at the field. "Did Ashley throw the ball really far for you?" he asks.

"Shoot, she had me running all over that field." Rosey gasps, as her tongue is hanging down to the ground trying to catch her breath at the same time. Ashley ruffles my fur as she looks at Ernie and me telling us that tomorrow will be our turn, if it is okay after my appointment with Dr. Rice.

CHAPTER 2

Meeting Dr. Rice

Ashley is going to visit a friend of hers while I am at the vets. Rosey and Ernie are told to kennel and they run and jump on the doghouse, as the lady closed the gate. They'll stay in the kennel until I get back home. They tell me that this is what they have to do when they are left at home by themselves. This is to keep them safe from maybe getting out the main gate to the street.

"Let's go, Chong," says the lady, as she leads me to the car. "Load up, Buddy." "Oh boy, oh boy, I love riding in the car." I am thinking as I hop in. I'm smiling and my stubby tail will not stop wiggling.

The lady says, "Settle down, we'll be at the animal hospital very soon."

I'm as excited as I can be just going for a ride. I don't care if we are going to the store, the vet's, or just a drive. This is truly the best. I lay in the back of the car and as we are going down the street, I see some kids on bikes. They are yelling and laughing at each other. I love kids, I'm thinking, as my mind drifts back to a time when there were little kids that played in the yard at my papa's. Sometimes they would roll around on the ground with me, squealing with delight. Their mom would open the door and yell,

"You, kids come in now, it's time to eat."

They would take off running into the kitchen, as the screen door banged behind them. My chain only went to the edge of the porch, and I would have to turn and go back and lay down in the shade. I would lay there and wonder if the kids were going to come back out and play with me some more.

"We're here now, let's go," the lady says, interrupting my daydream. We get out and she takes me over to a clump of Redwood trees, on the edge of the driveway so I can take care of business before going inside. There are so many smells around the trees left by other dogs before me, but I want the dog that comes along to know that I've been here, so I sniff all around until I find a spot that has not been marked yet. The lady says to me, "let's go Chong, or we'll be late for our appointment." as I finish leaving my message. We go inside. To the left of the door there's a big pad on the floor, and I am shown how to sit on it.

"Hold still!" the lady says softly, while she reads a dial on the wall that tells her how much I weigh. The scale says I weigh 74 lbs. This is not enough weight for a big Rottweiler like me; I should weigh between 90 to 130 lbs.

The receptionist at the desk gives the lady papers to fill out my information. When she learns my name, she starts to laugh. That's when the lady explains the story about my littermate named Cheech, and again it sounds like a joke. After one of the women at the desk gives me a treat, another comes out to tell us that it is time for our appointment, and leads us into a room. A nurse comes in and takes my temperature.

She says, "You look like a good boy." as she pulls a treat out of the cookie jar on the counter. I can't believe how my life has turned around; I am the luckiest dog in the whole world!

The nurse tells us that Dr. Rice will be in shortly. While we wait, the lady gently pets me, softly saying, "Chong, you're going to like your new vet."

The door opens, and in walks Dr. Rice. She has the biggest and brightest smile that I have even seen. She talks to the lady about my left front shoulder, and the leg that hurts me so much. Dr. Rice listens to my heart with her stethoscope. As she straightens back up, she says, "I want you to bring him back tomorrow. Can you have him here between 8 and 9? I want to x-ray his shoulder and leg. You can drop him off, and when he's ready we will give you a call to come get him." The lady nods her head, "Yes, we'll be here. Thanks, Sara."

Dr. Rice gives me a scratch on my ear as she turns and goes out the door, exiting the room as fast as she entered it. I really like her, even though she doesn't kick down with the cookies, as the others do. With that, we leave the examination room and when we pass the receptionist's desk, I get yet another cookie! I really like this place I'm thinking! Everybody is so nice to me.

According to Ernie it's past dinnertime when we get home. He's got an internal clock that lets him know exactly when it's time to eat. He also acts as if nobody has fed him for days. Dinner is the same as yesterday, with me in the kennel, away from the other dogs. When I'm done, the gate is opened and Ernie beats Rosey to my bowl. There are just a couple of bites left.

"Couldn't ya have left a little more" he complains to me? "That woman is starving me to death."

Sometimes the lady might not be at home or is doing something when it's time for dinner, and that worries Ernie a lot. Dinner time is set for 2:00 o'clock, so when his alarm goes off, he starts letting her know by jumping around, trying to get her attention. After bouncing back and forth without her noticing him, he then sits straight, staring in her direction. His eyes slowly close as if he's hypnotized or is praying for the Goddess of Dog-Food to open the bag of kibble and let it rain down on him. His dream is having his bowl over-flowing with endless food. Now Rosey knows not to get all stirred up, because dinner always happens eventually. Ernie wishes he were a cat like the one that lives here, because her bowl is always full. He tells me that her name is Lillie, and she has somehow trained the lady to keep her bowl filled to the top at all times. She also is not supposed to walk around to the other side of the countertop, but in her quiet cat-like ways will make it to the other side by the doorway, where using her paw, she knocks anything she can onto the floor. This way she gets the lady's attention. When she hears her coming, she scurries back to her bowl, staring at the lady, with a look that says. Could you please fill it to the top?

Ernie has been filling me in about the cat whom I still have not met face to face, (he tells me that she will decide when the time is right.) She has been keeping her eye on me, trying to figure out if it's safe to meet. I smell her scent, and know that she has been in and out of her cat door, which is in the wall of the hallway by the living room.

We are in for the evening, and the other dogs have picked a spot to curl up. I find a place nearby, and settle down. The lady is looking at something called a computer. She's searching for German names for dogs. There are a couple of names she says aloud, but goes back to looking some more. Suddenly she stops and looks at me with a big grin on her face. She says, "Hey, how does Quinn sound to you?"

"Quinn...? What's a Quinn?" I wonder. I like the sound of it. Then she says, looking at me,

"Quinn, yeah, that's a great name!" With that I start wagging my tail at her. I am saying to myself,

"Quinn... Hi, my name is Quinn." I really like this name, and besides nobody's going to think a name like Quinn is a joke.

It's time for us to go to bed. I am so ready. I'm tired from playing with the other dogs, and my trip to the vets. I limp down the stairs to my blanket. The medication doesn't seem to be working very well. It seems like the only time my leg doesn't bother me is when I'm running with my pals. I try to forget about it, and fall asleep, dreaming of what tomorrow will bring, and oh how I love my new name. There can't be a luckier or happier dog than me.

My appointment to go back to the animal hospital is early in the morning. I have to stay there most of the day. Ernie and Rosey are put in the kennel, and I get to go for another car ride. "Quinn, load up, let's go!" says the lady, as I jump in the car.

My new name makes me feel very proud, and I'm told it fits me perfectly. There have been some great Rottweilers before me with the name of Quinn. The lady tells me a story about a song that was written by Bob Dylan, called "The Mighty Quinn". I smile to myself, thinking, I have a new family, a new home, and a great new name. It all goes together so well. I am a happy guy. Humm, so I think from now on I will call the lady....my mom. I can tell by the way she treats the other dogs, the cat and me, that she loves us very much, and our safety and comfort are at the top of her priority list.

The ride to the animal hospital takes no time at all. I was just getting comfortable, when I hear my mom say that we're here. I would have liked the ride to last a little longer. Once again, I'm led over to the big Redwood trees to leave my message. This is just part of going to visit the vets; It's like wiping your feet before going inside. We are almost to the door, when I start to get excited, remembering yesterday and new friends I had met, and how nice it was getting all those treats. Just thinking about all of this makes my tail start to wiggle with delight. Inside my mom has me stand on the scale again. This time it says I weigh 75 lbs, and that makes her smile. Susan, the girl at the desk, greets me as she reaches into the treat jar, and says "Hi, Chong."

I smile to myself and give her a happy wag of my tail, as I hear my mom inform her that from now on I will be called Quinn. Handing me a treat, she smiles and says,

"Quinn! What a nice name that is!" Another lady named Erin is sitting behind the desk. She gets up and comes over to see me.

"I think Quinn is a much better name for you than Chong," she says, slipping yet another treat my way. I am a very happy boy, and so proud to be know as Quinn. Someone comes out from the back, and takes my leash, and starts to lead me away. Seeing what is happening I stop in my tracks.

"Hold on!" I want to yell, "Wait for my mom!" I turn back towards where she is standing, at the same time I am being pulled in the opposite direction. "It's okay Quinn," my mom says, "I'll be back later for you."

I wonder, because I am unsure of where I'm going, "What does this word later mean?"

I don't know this new person and I'm a little nervous about what's going to happen to me. I go to the back, into a kennel with a blanket on the floor. Next to me is another big dog. He tells me he's here for some tests. This is all very new to me. I don't know what tests are. Will they test me too? All I know is my mom's not here, and that I'm scared. Just because I'm a Rottweiler doesn't mean that I'm big and fearless.

Nearby is a large room, with some people working. All of a sudden, I see the woman, who is called Dr. Rice. I feel a little better now that I recognize her. The people in the room call her, Sara, like my mom. Therefore, I'm thinking, "I shall call her, Dr. Sara."

I hear her telling a man named Danny to get a blood sample from me, and also get me ready for x-rays of my shoulder and leg. She needs to see what's going on. Danny comes to take me out of the kennel into the large room. He says to me as he is opening the kennel gate,

"Come on Big Guy, we need to draw some blood for Dr. Rice." as he leads me over to the other side of the room.

Whatever that means must by okay, because he called me "Big Guy." I wag my stubby tail at him, letting him know this is fine with me. As I'm asked to lie down, a girl named, Hillary comes towards me.

"That's a good boy, Quinn."

She kneels on the floor next to me, petting and holding me still, while Danny takes a hold of my front leg and paw. He has something in his other hand. He starts to poke my leg with what I will soon learn is called a needle. This will draw my blood into a vial, for the vet to look at later. As soon as I feel that needle touch my skin I jerk away; I don't want any part of this. I give Danny my most serious and deepest grumbling growl, as I try to pull harder to get away from all of this. Danny puts his arm around my neck and lays on me, holding me to the floor. My mind is racing so very fast,

"This can't be the same place I was at yesterday, where everybody gave me treats and was so nice."

These guys are scaring the life out of me. I give out another serious growl:

"Grrrr." "They must know I mean business!" Danny looks around and says, "Gina, can you get a muzzle? We need to make sure he doesn't bite."

Gina slips the muzzle over my head and mouth. Never (until now) would I have thought about biting. It's not in my nature to do that. I normally love everyone I meet. However, in a situation like this….. "What's a guy suppose to do?"

Thoughts are racing through my mind so fast, as I give them one of the deepest growls I have saved up for a time like this. The muzzle holds my mouth shut, and now I get angry!

"Ouch, e-gads," I let out a yelp. That Danny has just stuck a needle in my leg. "I don't like this!" I mutter to myself, as I start to experience a strange and at the same time, fuzzy, warm feeling flow through my body.

"Why oh,…..Why….did …he… do… this.. to.. me?"……. Ohhhh,……….. I am now unconscious. In my sedated state of mind, I know nothing of what is going on with me, nor what is happening around me.

Denise, one of Dr. Sara's assistants, helps take the x-ray of my leg, and also one of my hips. Dr. Sara wants to make sure I don't have something called Hip Dysplasia, which my mom's other Rottweilers had. It's very painful. Dr. Sara has been my Mom's vet for so long, she figures my mom would want to know about my hips.

Quite some time has passed since I nodded off to dreamland and I'm beginning to wake up. I slowly open my eyes, and look around. I hear voices, and can make out blurry images across the room. My eyelids are heavy and I start to drift off to sleep again. While the sedative is wearing away, Dr. Sara shows my mom the x-rays. They both are happy at the way my hips look; There is not any problems. The news about my shoulder is not so good. there's arthritis invading the scapula, which causes extreme pain to my shoulder. There are bone spurs that rub the tendons and make me limp. It makes it look like one of my legs is shorter than the others.

I open my eyes half way, as I hear someone stop in front of the kennel. It's that guy, Danny, and he is slowly opening the gate. I'm not really sure if I want to go with him. But he gently says to me, "Come on big guy, your mom is waiting to take you home." My fuzzy mind is telling me, "That's the best news I've heard all day."

I'm excited about hearing that, but I'm pretty woozy, and my legs wobble when I try to walk. Danny takes me slowly out to the lobby, where Dr. Sara is talking to my mom about something. I can't hear what they're saying, but I'm so glad to see her. It doesn't show because I feel goofy still. We come out into the cool of the late afternoon, where she helps me into the car for the ride back home.

My favorite Vet, Dr. Sara

CHAPTER 3

GIVING DANNY TROUBLE

On the way home, I barely hear her telling me a story about the time she tripped over one of her daughter's dogs. She fell on her shoulder, and in doing so, chipped a bone. Because she didn't do anything about it, over the years arthritis had set in. So she has an idea of how badly this can hurt. Dr. Sara had told my mom about how she was going to have a knee replacement operation soon. When Dr. Sara saw her orthopedic doctor, he made a remark to her that her knee was the worst he had ever seen. In addition, he asked her how in the world she had endured the pain that she was experiencing. No one should have to go through chronic pain day after day, and week after week.

We are home now, and my legs still feel strange to me. I'm helped out of the car, and limp into the house on my own. I follow my mom into the kitchen, as she is getting ready to fix my dinner.

"So I hear you gave Danny some trouble today!" she says to me. "This isn't good or acceptable, Quinn." "I've been going to Dr. Rice for years, and none of my Rottweilers ever had to be muzzled."

I have no idea what her other dogs went through at the vets, but I know that she is not pleased with me. I really haven't been to the vet very much and I guess my manners are not what they are supposed to be. However, I do want to behave for her. She doesn't understand how very scared I was. I was also very confused about how different today was compared to yesterday.

"There will be a time when you will have to go back for another appointment. I think this next week I'll take you in for a visit with the girls at the desk, just so you can feel comfortable when you have to go there."

I'm listening to what she's saying, smiling to myself, remembering the treat jar on the counter.

"We can go to places like Rainbow Ag, and walk around and meet new friends. This way, you'll feel more comfortable in strange places."

She turns and faces me adding, "I want you to realize that most of the trips there won't be so bad. Heck, Quinn there were times when I had to go to my oncologist for chemo treatments and I never looked forward to doing that! Because I had to be hooked up to an IV for hours." I am listening to her telling me this, wondering what she's talking about.

"Chemo treatments, humm?" I hear the word treat, but the way she is saying it, I don't believe it's anything good. When the girls at the desk would say, "Want a treat, Quinn," I knew there was nothing bad about that. Therefore, when I have to go back I'll be a good boy. How can I not resist those delicious goodies they give out?

I liked the girls at the front desk, because they gave me the most treats of all. And that Danny guy was just trying to help me. I also liked Dr. Sara very much. I even tried to give her as big a smile as she gave me. I wasn't sure what they were doing to me, so I had to make them think that if I grumbled at them, they would leave me alone. I certainly didn't want them to know I was scared. I didn't know they were trying to help me. I was protecting myself by growling at them. It is my way of saying, "I don't like that, and you better stop!"

One night not long after I came to live here, I was lying at the bottom of the stairs, when my mom came down and sat on the stair above me. She was talking to me, stroking my back, and scratching behind my ears. I was eating it up, loving every minute of it. For some reason she wanted to rub my bad shoulder, the one that hurt me so very, very much. I didn't like her touching it, and let out a long, low grumble.

"Eh, Eh," she said, in the sternest tone I had ever heard from her. "We don't do that here!"

She looked so much taller to me, as she stepped up on to the next step up. "I will not have this attitude from you."

And she turned to go upstairs, leaving me there, wondering, "Why did she do that?"

I just wanted her to know that my shoulder hurt me really bad. I laid there for a while thinking about what had happened. I know grumbling at her was wrong. I limped up the stairs, into the living room and sat in front of her, and offer my paw, as I used to do to my papa. She took it, and said,

"Does this mean your going to be a good boy, Quinn, you can't be growling at me like that!" She says.

I put my head on her knee, and I look back at her with love. In that quick moment, our bond is set. She has shown me total respect and fair play. I knew from then on I wanted to do the same for her.

"Okay, my friend," She smiled, "I know you didn't mean it."

Looking at the clock, she said in a surprised voice, "No wonder you were grumpy, Quinn, it's time for your pain pill."

She goes to the front door, and calls Ernie and Rosey in for their last cookie of the night. Before giving them their cookies, she opens my mouth very wide and tucks my pill down in the back of my throat. Then we get our cookies. Those two gobble their cookies down but I don't like to eat like that. The food I ate before coming here was not tasty, so I want to enjoy every bite.

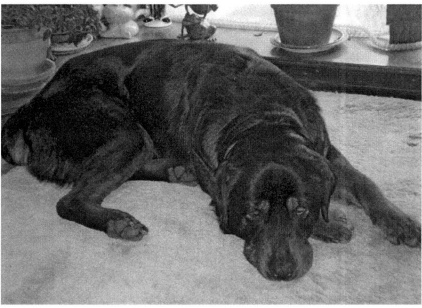

Relaxing by the front door

Rosie and me relaxing after playing. Ernie is up to something.

CHAPTER 4

QUINN'S BIRTHDAY PARTY

My mom was looking at some papers she got from the veterinarians, when she said, "Oh wow, Quinn, your birthday was two days after I brought you home. I guess when Sara called your other vet for your history file, this was on it." she added, smiling at me.

"Well, you know what that means tomorrow we will have to celebrate!" She says, giving me a wink of her eye. "You will all get a Frosty Paws ice cream cup," she smiled.

I find out later Frosty Paws is an ice cream treat for dogs. Wow! Another goody I never knew dogs got.

"And……….if you can stand it, I will sing Happy Birthday to you with Ernie howling along," she laughed.

"But don't expect Rosey to sing along, cause she doesn't do that." I am thinking, "I don't remember ever having a birthday party," Then pondering, "Do other dogs get parties for their birthdays?"

I trot out and down onto the lawn, and lay there thinking about a time at my papa's, when one of the little girls' had a birthday party. I remember the kids were running all over with funny hats on their heads, laughing and blowing noisemakers. They were having a great time, and I wanted to be off my chain, so I could play too. I would bark at them, to try to get their attention. Maybe if I barked enough, they just might come and let me into their game. Then I remembered someone came out the back door and yelled at me to stop barking. I turned away, and laid down on the cool cement of the walkway.

The next day, my mom comes out to the yard where the other two dogs and I are watching the two young cats through the chain link fence. They are crouched down under the boat that is parked in the driveway, along the other side. Ernie is barking wildly, and Rosey is barking just as bad. They are letting those cats know that if they could, they would be through that fence, chasing them up a tree or down to the creek. I stand there watching, not barking, waiting to see what the cats are going to do. Some days I limp over to the fence, and find a good spot, so as I can catch them playing. They usually are rolling around, jumping and chasing each other. Just as I wish to be friends with Dakota, I would want that with them. If that were so, they could come to my party. My mom calling to us interrupts my thoughts. "Hey you guys, I've got something for you."

We race over to where she is opening three small paper cups of doggy ice cream. As soon as she puts each one down in front of us, we start licking the soft, creamy treat. Boy, this is so delicious, who would of thought there would be ice cream for dogs?

Ernie is almost done, and is chewing on the cup, making sure he will not leave even one drop. Rosey is not very far behind. I'm licking mine slowly, taking my time, when Ernie starts yelling at me.

"Hey, you'd better give me the rest of that." as he's staring at my cup. "How come you're taking so long to finish?"

"It tastes so good, I want to enjoy all of it," I say, in between licks, "I never had Frosty Paws before."

Rosey has her cup chewed in a few pieces, so my mom comes down to the lawn and picks up the mess that is now blowing across the yard. She comes over to where I'm laying on the grass and sits down next to me. In her hand is a new dog brush.

"Happy Birthday Quinn, this is for you," she says. And with that, she starts brushing my coat. I smile to myself thinking how great that feels. I lay quietly along side of her as she is telling me how glad she is to have found me, and what a wonderful dog I am. At the same time, I'm thinking, I've got to be the luckiest dog in the world. And oh what a nice day it is turning out to be.

While brushing my coat she starts telling me a story of how Ernie came to live here with her. Ernie had two sisters that didn't look like him at all. They had docked tails and the markings of Jack Russell

Terriers. Because this breed was very popular at the time, the sisters were adopted right away. Nobody paid any attention to Ernie, who was just a little orangey-red hound-like dog. When my mom was visiting where he lived, she would always stop and give him a pat on the head. Then she would go into the house, and he would go back under the root of the big Bay tree next to the porch.

My mom told me that not too long before Ernie was born, she had to put her first Rottweiler down. He was six months short of turning twelve years old. He had gotten very sick, and had bone cancer, called osteosarcoma. Because she needed to fill the vacant spot that was left by the loss of her best buddy, she took Ernie and brought him home. She wanted to give him a good home, because she knew Ernie would certainly end up being tied to a tree in Willits somewhere. She didn't want that to happen to him. As she continued the story, I was thinking,

"Humm, I don't know where Willits is, but I sure know what it's like being tied up."

She finishes the story and gets up to go back in the house. I'm smiling, as I think about the story she just told me. "Boy, what a lucky break Ernie got, just like me."

Every morning we go out into the yard, and that's when I notice that it must have rained during the night, as the grass is very damp under my feet. Droplets of rainwater fall on my nose from the bare branch on the big Catalpa tree next to the kennel. Rosey told me that in the spring, this tree has huge, heart-shaped leaves, eight by twelve inches wide, with beautiful white clusters of flowers, with yellow centers. The fruits of this tree are long beans. It's a great shade tree for a kennel. There is a very cold wind blowing across the yard. I step lightly over the lawn, looking and sniffing for a spot to call mine. Another cold winter day has settled in Ukiah; the city I now call home. Sleeping inside at night is wonderful. At my papa's house, I got to sleep in the shed, and that was okay because I didn't get wet when it rained. But it wasn't as warm as sleeping inside a house with a warm fire, and the cold was hard on my shoulder and leg, because of the constant pain I felt. As the day warmed up, the pain would get better, but some days were worse than others. I can't remember exactly what I did to make it hurt, but it's been like this for a very long time.

In the morning, we are called in for cookies, which are gobbled right up. Then Ernie and Rosey are sent back out, so my mom can fix my breakfast with Metacam, the liquid medication, she's giving me. Now, as I'm finishing my breakfast, I see the cat up close. She has been so very quiet, securely perched in the window box above the kitchen sink, watching me. So, this is the infamous cat named Lillie! I give her a quick wiggle of my tail, and nod hello to her. Her eyes go into narrow slits as she takes in the sight of me, and my mom at the sink. She is the most beautiful cat I have ever laid eyes on. And at the same time, the only cat that has been this close to me.

She looks like she is ready for Halloween, because she is orange and black with white paws, and white around her neck, and chest. Her body is the color of orange and black all mixed together, like she had rolled around in these two colors, and they blended together, making her coat look blotched like the color of calico. The spots by her mouth and nose look like they were dipped it in a bowl of milk, with a little bit of butterscotch pudding mixed in. I like the way she is marked, with one black ear and the other orange. She looks at me, as she slowly rises up into a huge arc. Doing so reveals a white tummy. I also notice that one of her back legs is black and the other one is orange, just like her ears. But they are opposite from the other. She has an interesting mark under one of her eyes, it looks like a teardrop. I like the way that looks. I think that there aren't too many cats around with markings as unique as hers.

For sometime my mom had been looking for a new cat. Her friend, Jane, at the animal hospital where I go, had been fostering a litter. One day at the hospital, Jane motioned to my mom to come in back and see the kittens. After watching them for a little bit, Lillie was the one she picked out. Her full name is "Lillie-Billie-Boop-Bop" And when my mom goes outside to call her, she yells, "Lillie-Billie, Lillie-Billie, Billie, here kitty-kitty here kitty-kitty!"

Then Lillie comes a running. My mom tells me that Lillie came to live with her about the same time as Rosey did. They're the same age. When Lillie was a kitten and Rosey a puppy, they would roll around on the living room floor. Now that they are four years old, Rosey is a whole lot bigger than Lillie. They still play together, and because of the size difference, Rosey can put Lillie's head in her mouth. Lillie will swat at Rosey with her two front paws. She keeps her claws in as long as Rosey is gentle with her. Lillie will hide behind a chair and wait for Rosey to walk by, and then leap on to Rosey's front leg, or with her paws hang off her chest. Sometimes they get going at each other kind of hard. That's when I start to get excited and want to join in, but Ernie tells me that it's not a good idea.

He says, "Lillie would not like you getting that close, because you would scare her." I'm confused, "Why does she let Rosey play hard like that, and not me?" Ernie gives me a look, like boy, you don't listen. "Don't you remember what I told you about the Rottweiler breaking her jaw?" "Oh, un huh, I guess I forgot." I answered him. "But I would never hurt her."

"Well your going to have to take your time," Ernie says, "Just let her check you out first."

Ernie goes on to explain about how his ancestors are a hunting breed. The terrier is great at getting rats or varmints. It's called "going to ground" among the Terrier people. He has gotten a few rats from under the ivy on the fence. And how proud he was, after showing my mom his kill. He went on to say that when Rosey and Lillie start playing rough, he has a hard time controlling his prey drive. He continues telling me how Terriers are bred to hunt and chase down prey. They also like to stir up trouble whenever they can. Ernie's so very good at this. He is constantly getting Rosey in trouble. Rosey's background is a breed that works with sheep, herding them. Border Collies are smart, because they have to help keep the flock safe. They think for themselves. This makes Rosey bossy at times.

When Ernie and Rosey have been up at the gate barking at the dogs walking their humans by, they will stop barking and start fighting. My mom will come out the door and call them by name. But they act like they don't hear her, and continue fighting. I know they can hear her.... because I sure can.

She sounds like she means business, so when I hear my name called, there is nothing more that I want to do, than run down the driveway to where she is standing on the porch. She always gives me a hug and a big smile and says,

"What a good boy you are, Quinn," while ruffling the fur on my neck. She turns, looking up the driveway and yells,

"Hey, That's enough," as the two race each other down the driveway as fast as they can run. They really would like to get out, and take off down the street to the ball-field.

My friend Sophie

CHAPTER 5

OUTSIDE THE GATE

This reminds me of the night some friends came to visit my mom. After parking in the driveway, they came through the gate. The last one through didn't latch the lock well enough. Even though it looked like it was secure, just a little bit of wind made the gate slowly swing open. Rosey was the first to notice. She called to Ernie and me,

"Hey you guys, look, the gate's open! Let's go down to the lower field, where we can run."

She yelled over her shoulder, as she took off running. Ernie looked at the open gate, and let out a yip.

"Come on, Quinn, let's go!" He reminded me about the great smells out there; like when my mom would take me for a walk, it was so much fun sniffing out the news left by other dogs that had come by. So I didn't think that would be so bad of a thing to do, and I would be with them.

Rosey and I started down the street, when Ernie said, "Hey guys, let's go up and around the corner and down to the creek, where we can really have some fun."

I was following Rosey, where we were sniffing in front of Dakota's house. Ernie kept bugging Rosey about going the other way, but she was not paying any attention to him. At the same time I wasn't sure whether to continue going along with this. It sounded like quite the adventure, but then it occurred to me that maybe this was something that wasn't supposed to be happening without our mom here.

Ernie was anxious to take off and go up the street when instead he turned and ran back down the driveway towards the house, yelling at us,

"I'm gonna tell mom, that you guys are out in the street!"

He laughed, and in a sing-song kind of chant he said, "Ya gonna get in trouble, ya gonna get in trouble."

That was when Rosey hastily said, "We better get back inside the gate, before mom catches us out here, cause she'll be angry."

"Oh, no!" I'm thinking, starting to panic a bit. I really don't want to be yelled at, especially when this wasn't my idea. It's darker now than when we first got out here; and Rosey just started running before I could turn around. And I can't see which way she went. There are two driveways made out of asphalt, separated by a chain link fence. They look exactly alike to me, but which one did Rosey take? I start down the first one I see.

"Ohhhh, no," I whine to myself. Through the wire of the fence, I can see my mom almost at the gate opening; and Rosey is right there where I can see her now. She of course is on the other side, which is the right driveway. I slink-down into a 'Marma-duke' like slither, heading to who knows where? What was I thinking, listening to that Ernie? I hear my mom, in a soft tone of voice that let's me know its okay, as she says to me, "Hey, Buddy, over here. It's all right, Quinn."

With that I quickly spin around and head towards the right driveway. Rosey is already down to the porch. Whew, I don't want to be in that kind of situation again, I'm thinking, as I'm getting a scratch behind my ear. I feel a whole lot better now, as I hear her say, "I bet you could go for a cookie, right fella?"

I followed my mom down the driveway and into the house, where Ernie was giving me a look as if he had never done anything wrong. He had been the one that had run back into the house, acting like Rosey and I were the only ones that were bad. I could tell by the way my mom was looking at me, she knew exactly what was what. She knows us very well. Shaking her head at Ernie, she praised Rosey and me for not running off. I knew she was relieved that she didn't have to go looking for us, and at the same time, wasn't too pleased at the person, who so carelessly left the gate unsecured.

I've been playing with the other two dogs everyday, learning the ins and outs of how I'm expected to behave around here.

My weight is slowly increasing. The medication my mom puts in my food has helped reduce the pain in my shoulder. Everyday I am reminded about how to sit and down when told. I am the best boy on a leash, walking on the left side of my mom. Things should be settling down soon. Each day is wonderful here, especially being off that awful chain. My mom takes us out on the lawn and throws our toys for us to chase. When Ernie's yellow rubber bone is tossed, he runs and gets it. But he doesn't bring it back to her; instead he holds it in his mouth making it squeak, running around like the funny clown he is. With his bone in his mouth he bounces all over the lawn trying to make us miss catching our toys.

Rosey's toy is the blue T-Rex dinosaur. She is so fast, she is back before my ball even gets thrown. Also Rosey is demanding, expecting the toy to be thrown for her again before my turn. I run out after my ball, and grab it up, turn and run back and drop it. My mom is so busy with Rosey that she has to kick my ball instead of throwing it. When it is dropped in front of her, she will pretend to kick it one way, and then quickly kick it the other way. I drop down on my front legs, rocking back and forth with my butt up in the air. I'm trying to figure which way she's going to kick it. I love this game even though it's tricky. It's more fun than just running after the ball. And OH, how I'm crazy about that. The whole time we're playing, the toys are making the squeaky sound and Dakota can hear this on the other side of the fence. He doesn't like us making all this racket, and is barking like a madman. This goes on until my mom can tell that we're getting tired. She stops the play until later in the afternoon, when it gets cooler.

I start grinning when the camera comes out.

CHAPTER 6

Dog Class

Today my mom tells me we are going to dog class. She gets the leather leash off the hook by the front door. Her friend, Sandy Hoyt, and Sandy's husband, Ray, teach dog obedience classes. My mom smiles at me and says, "It's fun, and you can meet some new dog friends."

Ernie and Rosey are called to the kennel, where they go to settle in. They aren't too happy, about being left behind. Ernie whines, "Gee, Quinn, you get to do all the fun things"

"Gosh, I haven't done anymore fun things than you have, the only other fun thing, was riding to the vet's in the car."

"That's what I'm talking about! You get to go in the car and I don't." I looked at him and said, "Well, maybe she'll take you next time!" I turn and run up the stairs, across the porch into the carport, where my mom is waiting for me.

"Load up, Quinn, we've got to go." I settle in the back of what I am beginning to think of as my car. I do remember hearing my mom say one time, "This is Quinn's car!"

We head out towards the north end of town where there is a big building and my mom pulls into the huge parking lot. She lets me out to take care of business before going inside. I'm walking along side of her as we get to the doorway. She stops and gives a quick pull up on the leash, as she says, "Sit!" While I'm trying to stretch my neck out as far as I can to look inside. Again, she says sternly, "Quinn, sit!" This time I do what I'm told.

When I finally get my head inside, I see a tunnel stretched out in the middle of the floor, a jump ring, and some weave poles. I wonder what could those things be for? Suddenly, I hear someone talking to my mom from the table by the doorway. "Oh, MT, what a nice guy, you have there," Sandy says.

"Thanks," says my mom, grinning proudly. As they talk back and forth, I wonder what's an MT? I haven't heard that before. Now I'm a very smart dog, and as I listen, I realize that MT is the person I call my mom. That's okay, cause I'm going to call her my mom. I don't feel comfortable calling her anything else! We go inside and find a good spot at the edge of the room. There's a workbench behind where we are standing, facing the middle of the room. I detect an enticing smell coming from up on the bench top. It smells like cheese. And I recognize the smell of hot dogs. Maybe if I'm good at what I'm supposed to be doing, I'll get rewarded with some of those goodies. Soon other dogs and their people start to arrive, I stick out my nose to greet them and wag my tail back and forth really fast. My mom looks down and smiles at me proudly. She likes the way I want to meet new friends. That makes me happy. Everybody finds their place around the edge of the room, and then a man very quietly walks to the middle of the room, and introduces himself.

"Hi, my name is Ray, and this is Sandy. This is 'The Ukiah School for Dogs' and this class is for your dog to learn how to be obedient. Well, it's really for you to learn how to teach your dog how to mind you. So maybe we should call it the dog school for people." He jokes. Then he sounds serious saying, "You will learn how to train your dog to mind you."

After Ray talks, Sandy tells us about other things that we have to learn. My mom told me that she brings her dogs here to let them meet new friends, while learning good manners at the same time. She already knows how to train a dog for obedience.

Next thing I know, we're starting out the door, one at a time. A good dog always stops with his person at the doorway and sits, waiting to be told, "Heel", before he goes out the door. And a very good dog never lunges ahead of the person. When we get outside, we start heeling along the side of our person, going at the same pace. First we walk normally, then faster. Just when I start getting used to this, we are told to go slow; so slow it feels like I'm ready to sit, but my mom keeps me moving, and then it's back to a normal walk. We go around in a big circle a couple of times, then Sandy tells us to "Halt." We stop, sit, then we start again. After that we stand in a straight line facing the other line of dogs about 10 feet across from us. We then walk towards the opposite side going through the lineup. I like this, and I love all the other dogs. Some of them are friendly, mostly the younger ones. Some are not very good with other dogs and this is one of the reasons that they're in this class. I love getting to go to dog class because I get to be with my mom.

My mom told me a story about her first Rottweiler, Morton. She worked with a dog trainer from Petaluma, walking the streets downtown, going in and out of stores, passing other dogs along the sidewalk. He was learning how to heel and watch, my mom trusting that she would not walk him into a wall! This is where she first learned how to train for competition in the Obedience ring. The lessons were very serious one-on-ones. After working once a week with the trainer, she would work Morton every day, and then showed him in obedience trials at dog shows. The reason why I'm telling you this is because she wants to get a special number called a PAL/ILP from the American Kennel Club for me, so I could compete in the trials. The PAL/ILP is for purebred dogs like me that were in a litter that was not registered. Most pure bred litters are registered with the AKC. When the dogs reach six months old they can be entered and shown in the Conformation ring. Usually when they show in the Obedient ring they start around the age of two to three years old. It takes at least three trials of a qualifying score of 170 to a perfect score of 200 to get a CD title. CD meaning companion dog. That is when the dog knows all about the basic commands of "Heel", "Sit", "Stay", "Down", and "Come'. And if one wants to go on to higher training, there is CDX meaning companion dog excellence, where the dog does all the commands off leash and jumps the broad and high jumps and brings back the dumb-bells and UD, meaning utility dog, where they do all of the things named along with getting a scented article and glove. Then UDX, meaning utility dog excellence. She said that it would be so much fun, and I'm all about having fun. Heck I just turned eight years old, and didn't get to do half the stuff I'm doing now. It's so great doing things with my mom, and my new pals

Ernie and Rosey. Things are different since I moved in with my new family. I've definitely got to be the luckiest dog in the whole world.

After class, my mom takes me through the tunnel. I'm not too sure about it, but I know that she wouldn't put me in any danger so I went on through. She met me at the end and praised me. "What a good boy, Quinn," she tells me smiling, and slips me a treat. She shows me the ring. I'm not sure if I was supposed to go through it, around it, or under it. She wants me to go through it, and uses her hands to guide me through. I come back around in front of the ring and she motions with her hand towards it again. I know how to do this now, so as she tells me, "Quinn, over."

I jump through again, and I get praised *and* another treat. Man, I'm having so much fun trying out this obstacle course, and learning how to be a good and obedient dog. I didn't know that dog class could be anything like this.

When we get home, my mom is telling us that a dog named Annie is coming to stay with us for a few days. Rosey smiles, and says that she likes it when Annie is here. Ernie is jumping all around like a total nut. He loves Annie. So, I'm wondering who is this Annie, and what is she like? The two of them give me a little run-down about her. First off, Ernie says to me,

"Oh Quinn, Annie is part Rottweiler, just like you. But she has a long tail, and a little bit of white on her. The tan dots above her eyes are a dead give-a-way for the Rottweiler part. And she is like Rosey's size."

He goes on to say that she was a shelter dog.

"What's a shelter dog?" I ask.

Rosey butts in saying, "It's a dog that someone gives up for one reason or another."

"Or runs away and gets lost." adds Ernie.

Some are lucky and find good homes to live out their lives with a new family or a person that will give them lots of love and take care of them. There are lots of old dogs in shelters that nobody wants; for no other reason than that they are old. The Rottweiler that came to live with us before you was eight years old, and very arthritic. She spent most of her life chained under a trailer in Northern Arizona somewhere, during the heat of summer and the cold of winter.

Our mom was on the computer looking for a Rottweiler to adopt, when she found the ad for this old girl. It said that she might be a great dog for an older couple, who like to sit around and watch TV. And because my mom was going through her chemo treatments at that time, she figured this would be a great match. After emailing back and forth, telling the foster person about her life with Rotties, they knew that Jazz would have a great home.

As Ernie is telling me this story about Jazz, I realize it is a lot like my story. He said he heard my mom telling someone one day that this is what she would do from now on; that she was an old lady that would take in old dogs. Ernie said,

"She ain't really *that* old, cause she can still get us down and around through Anton's ball-field; and past the park, back up Standley St in a half hour. And besides in dog years, I'm older than she is."

Rosey reminds Ernie to finish about Annie.

"Please tell me the rest of the story, Ernie." I beg him.

"Well this really neat family met Annie at the Humane Society out in Redwood Valley. They liked her and decided to adopt her. Since they knew our mom from dog-sitting their first Rottweiler, they would ask her sometimes if she could dog sit Annie. That's how we got to know her.

"I'm looking forward to meeting her," I say. "She sounds like she's nice."

"Oh yeah, she loves it when we all get out there and play ball." Rosey says.

Later on in the afternoon the telephone rings. When my mom is through talking, she comes outside to let us know that Annie is on her way. Ernie starts getting excited, and races up to the gate to be the first one to greet her. Rosey goes and jumps back up on to the doghouse on the porch to lie back down where she was. I just stand there, wondering if Annie will like me. I already know I like her, just because I like every dog or person I meet.

Soon a big white SUV pulls into the driveway. When it stops, out jump two girls and a tall pretty lady. One of the girls has a leash holding Annie, who is pulling hard towards the gate. Annie seems like she can't wait to get through it, and is smiling a great big doggie smile. After trotting up to greet them, I stand back, watching the bunch of them making their way through the gate, trying to bring all of Annie's stuff in with them, at the same time not letting Ernie or Rosey slip out. They have her food, and dishes, along with her bed. My mom and the lady, who is called Erin exchange hellos and hugs, as they start down the driveway.

Rosey and Ernie are all over this poor dog, as they welcome her. She gives me a sniff, as I do her.

"And just who are you, handsome?" She asks me, with a wink.

"Hi, my name is Quinn!" I say back to her.

"The other dogs told me that you come and stay sometimes with them. And your name is Annie."

"Yes I do, and it's nice to meet you, Quinn," she smiles at me.

"Is that right about you being adopted from a shelter? I was adopted, and feel like the luckiest dog in the world. And it's nice to meet you too, Annie, they told me all about you." I say as I sniff at her again.

Ginger, the dog next door

CHAPTER 7

BUMP ON MY FOOT

As I listen to Annie tell her story about her family, my mind starts to drift off, and I realize that being adopted, was the best thing that ever happened. I love being part of my new family, not being chained, and able to run all over the yard chasing my pals, and also learning how to be friends with Lillie. The closest she has been to me was just the other evening. I was sitting next to the edge of the couch, listening to a story my mom was telling me about how she loved her dogs, and all the things she did with them. I was shaking hands with her, when Lillie batted her paw at my leg. I looked at her and knew that she was beginning to accept me little by little. I noticed that she wasn't as jumpy around me, when I would come trotting by her. She still gives herself some room for escape when she's near me. But as always she is on the alert with any dogs, because of her jaw accident.

I'm learning about my new home. The pets that live around us in the nearby yards. How we have doggie guests that stay with us from time to time and that there are critters that reside in the bushes in the back-yard. When Ernie or Rosey get a whiff of an odor from one of them, they want to take off and run the fence-line. At night an old raccoon comes around, looking for something to eat. He thinks he can get to our food that is kept in a metal garbage-can on the front porch. He never gets the lid off.

It's night now, and we are lying in our favorite spots, when all of a sudden, Rosey jumps up and trots over to the cat door, smelling outside. She catches a scent, turns and runs to the window next to the front door. Then she spots the raccoon, all the while barking and scratching at the glass. Ernie wastes no time, racing over to Rosey. Pushing her aside, he crashes right into the window. He's very excited,

"Mom, Mom, let us out!!" He's barking at her, "We've got to chase him away!" As Rosey scratches the door to get out, she's yelling, "He's on the porch…let us out!"

My mom jumps up and hurries to the door and unlocks it, as she pushes it open. They charge out, banging into each other, flying off the porch into the night.

Annie was lying over by the stairs, so it took her a little longer getting to the front door, where she also took off running. I just stand next to my mom, staring with her into the dark towards the direction they ran. As fast as they left, they come running back. Their tongues hanging out of their mouths, panting hard. Ernie is all jazzed as he tells me how they were so close to getting that old raccoon. They don't like him at all. This is our property and he has no business hanging out here. Especially when he's trying to steal our food.

The next day my mom takes me for a walk down to the end of our street which leads to a couple of Little League fields. Rosey told me that the little field is where Ashley takes her. On the big field kids are playing baseball. My mom leads me over to the fence, where we stop and watch. Oh how I wish that I could go and run with those kids. They look like they are having so much fun. We stand there for just a little bit, and then continue down through the big parking lot. Along the Parks Dept. building are big fat steel posts, and my mom helps me weave in and out of the posts, like when we were at dog class, where she showed me how to weave in and out of the skinny ones that are like broom handles.

After making my way through the posts, we walk along the bushes at the edge of the parking lot. There are all kinds of smells. I notice that there are some birds that live among the branches, as they flutter and fly out. We get to the street, where I'm told to sit as a car comes racing down past us.

She says, "Quinn, you have to sit at the corners before we cross the street."

She's always telling me about how things are in the big world, outside our main gate. She worries that something bad will happen to the other dogs and me.

We're in the City Park now, and lots of little kids are playing on the playground equipment. They're having the best time. My mom takes me over to one of the benches near them. As she sits down, she tells me, "Quinn, sit!" I do what she says, as I'm wagging my stubby tail, watching the kids. They make me happy, so I smile at them; hoping one will come over and pet me. All of a sudden this little toddler comes waddling very fast towards me. His mother isn't happy at all. In her mind, I look like the big bad wolf, who might grab her baby. She has a look of pure panic on her face, as she's trying so hard to catch up to him and swoop her child up and away from danger. My mom informs her that it's okay, as the baby is right in my face and I give him a big slurp of a kiss on the side of his. She tells the mother, "He loves little kids, and wouldn't hurt them."

The woman lets out a big sigh of relief, as she says, "I have to keep my eye on him every minute."

The baby is banging on my back with his little fists, but I don't mind, cause it reminds me of when I was at my papa's and the little kids would do the same thing. I loved it when they would include me in their games.

We get back home and I go inside and lay down. My mom takes Annie, Ernie and Rosey outside to throw the ball up the driveway for a little bit. They're waiting for Annie's mom to come get her, and take her home. Just about the time when they are done playing is when Erin comes with her girls to pick up Annie. I had fun with her and hope she can come back and stay with us again. After Annie is gone my mom comes back into the house. She sits down on the carpet and leans against the couch, and proceeds to pet me. As she goes over my legs and feet, she notices a funny little bump on one of my back feet.

"*OH NOOO!*" she let's out a scream, and jumps up. I have no idea what has upset her so. She reaches down and touches it lightly.

"This can't be!" she gasps, as she goes into the kitchen, I'm confused, and follow her. I want to offer her my paw-- this will make everything better.

"Not another one!" She says, thinking about her other Rottweiler, who had a bump like mine.

She has me a little worried, by the way she sounds. She had as much fun as I did going for a walk, but now she acts like I did something wrong. She's not at all happy like earlier. She hurries past me and goes into another room. I lay down with Ernie and Rosey. I ask them if they know what's wrong? They say they don't have any idea. It's when she comes back into the living room, she looks like she's been crying.

In the morning she's on the phone, calling the vet's office for an appointment. I hear her telling the person on the other end that she found a bump on my foot, and it needs to be looked at right away. "Okay," she says, "I'll have him there in the morning."

The next day, we are off to the vet. All I know is that I get to go for a car ride. Yeah! This is good, I'm thinking, not even worrying about this silly little bump on my foot. We get there, and go inside to the scale by the door. My mom makes me stand on the scale, as she reads that I now weigh 84 lbs. Boy, does that make her smile. Seeing this makes me happy. Also I see my friend Erin at the desk, as she says,

"Hi, Quinn how about a treat," at the same time asking,

How much did I weigh?

"He weighs 84 lbs, and that's so cool!" my mom answers proudly.

It's been almost three months since I was weighed, and I'm putting on weight slow and steady. At first my mom wanted me to be up to the right weight faster than this. But she knows that wouldn't be good for the arthritis in my shoulder. I have been underweight for so long, the extra pounds have to be put on slowly.

We sit down in the lobby waiting for the nurse to call us into one of the examination rooms. Terry opens the door and motions to my mom that she wants us to come where she is. She smiles at me, and turns to the treat jar, taking one out and hands it to me. I like her right away. She takes my temperature and says Dr. Rice will be in shortly. I look at my mom, and she looks worried. Soon the door opens, and in comes Dr. Sara. I am happy to see her again. She and my mom exchange greetings, smiling at each other.

Dr. Sara asks, "What's going on?" as my mom shows her my left back foot that has a blister-like bump between the two middles toes. Neither one of them look happy, Nor am I happy at what is about to happen to me. Dr. Sara leaves the room, and within a couple of minutes nurse Terry comes and takes me down the hall to the big room. They're trying to hold me still, but I'm not going for this at all. Two of the staff manage to lift me up onto the table.

"Ohhhh, ouch!"

I look away, trying to think of something, anything, but what is going on. I can't help myself and give out a low rumble of a growl. It's like they don't hear me. I *really* want this to stop. They try to talk to me, telling me that it will be okay, as I feel that darn muzzle being slipped over my nose again. I'm shaking my head back and forth, trying to get it off. I know this not going to get any better, so I really start growling louder now. "Grrrrr!! Stop!!"

"Quinn, easy now, hang on. This will just take a second," Dr. Sara tries to assure me. I'm so mad now because they are not stopping. And then there that quick, stinging feeling in the muscle of my hip again, that I don't like. "Ohhhh,....I am feeling all goofy, and can't put up a struggle anymore. As the sound of their voices ever so slowly fade away...... After the sedative starts working, Dr. Sara sticks a needle into the swelling between my toes. She looks at the sample from the needle under a microscope, and from what she sees; it looks like it's an abscess forming, from possibly a puncture from a sticker or something sharp that I stepped on.

Time passes by as the sedative wears off, and soon I start to wake up. Dr. Sara calls to me that it's time to get up and go see my mom, where she is waiting for me out in the lobby. As I get to the end of the reception desk, I see my mom standing there looking towards me. She smiles as Dr. Sara walks me over to her.

"Wow, he looks messed up!" says my mom, wondering what's wrong with me.

"We had to sedate him, but he'll be fine in a while." She says, with a smile. "He was a bit of a grumbler today."

My mom shakes her head in a very disapproving look. She gets some antibiotics for me, then thanks Terry and we head for the door. Boy am I glad that's over. I shouldn't have growled like I did. As angry as I was, I tried very hard not to do it. But that bump between my toes is really sensitive and tender. And I just couldn't hold it back. We are back home now, and I feel a lot better. I trot up onto the porch and come inside.

Ernie asks me, "How'd it go today at the clinic?"

"Oh wow Ernie, those girls on the front desk are so nice to me. I love them, cause they always give me treats. And I know they think that I'm a nice boy. But I don't know why the ones in the big room have to hurt me by sticking me in the leg with those sharp needles. It makes me so mad! I gave the loudest growls I can, but it didn't stop them from hurting me with those darn needles. Today it wasn't my leg, but this blister that's popped up on my foot. I can't believe that my friend, Dr. Sara, took a needle and stuck me there. I tried not to growl at her, I hate to do that. But then they put that muzzle on me and I really got angry, big time. I felt the needle stick me, and that's the last I remember, until I woke up."

"Hey, Dude, you're a big tough Rottweiler who acts like the biggest chicken I have even known," Ernie snickers back at me. "I'm half your size, and I let them stick me with needles!'

I look at him with surprise and at the same time, I question him. "Doesn't it hurt you when they do that, and don't you get mad at them? I just want to be anywhere else besides there."

"You've got to bite the bullet, Quinn, and stop being such a wimp!"

"What do you mean, by this bite the bullet?"

"It means, Big Guy, you have to grow up, and take what's dished out to you like a *real* Rottweiler would."

Ernie's looking at me, like he can't believe that I'm such a baby.

"I know a little Chihuahua, dude, who lets them give him shots, when he needs them. Even I let them give me my annual shots, because this is what is expected from all dogs when they go see their veterinarians."

"You mean that all the other dogs let them do that?"

"Remember, Quinn when our mom said to you that none of her other Rottweilers ever had to be muzzled or held down? I'm just a little guy and let them stick me with needles when I go there, 'cause I sure like the cookies they give me. And besides, they think I'm the cutest little red dog they've ever seen."

Rosey has been laying on the carpet over by the wooden chest in the living room, listening to us talking. She raises her head up and looks at me, like I'm a big baby.

"Well, you big mama's boy, I'm a girl and I don't give them any trouble when I have to go see my vet." she then looks at me, and starts laughing,

"Suck it up Quinn, you big sissy!"

These guys are being so mean to me; I can't believe that they are talking to me like this. I would never say these things to them.

The whole time Ernie and Rosey are ripping into me, Lillie is perched up on the arm of the couch. With her eyes in thin slits, she adds her two cents, about how that other Rottweiler broke her jaw. She goes on to tell me how Dr. LaRue had to wire her chin with a little shirt button under it. She had to stay in the hospital for a long time, away from home, because my mom was going through chemo treatments at the time. Lillie was going to need medication given to her, and she might have accidentally scratched my mom. She's telling me how they had to stick her with needles, and she didn't even think about sinking her claws into the doctors' arm, or anybody else's for that matter. She was so shook up from what had happened. She also told me that the doctors at the hospital were all wonderful. That their job was to make the sick or injured pets that came in there better, and sometimes it didn't seem that way, but it was always for the best

Now I remember the girl at my papa's house saying that it was for the best when they let me come live here with my new family. I go over and lay down in the hallway by the living room. I'm thinking about my day at the vets, and what the other two dogs and Lillie were saying to me. I think about our ages, and the difference is four years. Yeah, Rosey's four, and has gone to the vets about twice a year. She seems just fine with it. I'm eight, and Ernie's almost 12 years. Those guys have been going to the vets all of their lives. I only remember going a couple of times, and I think they just stuck a needle in my back for a shot of some kind. Humm, I'm going to have to ponder this some more.

I am a happy guy. Notice my wrapped foot.

CHAPTER 8

HAVING FUN WITH ERNIE AND ROSEY

It's time for us to settle in for the night, and curl up on our blankets. I notice as I get my blanket all bunched up on one side, and snuggle in, my foot hurts. Rats, first my leg hurts, and now my foot hurts. What's going on? I'm thinking that the only thing worse would be if I was back sleeping in the shed. I don't think papa or the girl would have noticed anything wrong. I don't even want to think of what that would be like. I may not like it when one of my friends at the vets starts to do whatever they have to do to me, but I'm beginning to understand, kind of what Ernie and the other two were talking about.

The sun's up and it's still early in the morning, when my mom takes us outside to play ball. She has been giving me my pain medication in my breakfast, and it has been helping control the aching feeling in my shoulder. Also my foot doesn't seem to hurt as much either.

We start our game, running back and forth chasing toys, our mom throws for us. At the same time, I hear Dakota barking through the fence. Ernie drops his little yellow rubber bone and runs to the gap and starts clawing at the hole in the ivy, giving Dakota a bad time.

"Ha ha, Dakota we get to play and you don't,"

He says jumping around. "Nanner, nanner, you can't get me!"

He laughs, teasing as he runs back to continue playing his own game of catch me if you can. He growls in a fun way as he squeaks his toy. Dakota keeps on barking at us, in kind of an angry, scary, almost jealous way that lets us know he's not at all happy, and at the same time he can't play like we do. I never hear his family playing with him.

So instead he barks at us while pacing along the fence, until his mom comes out telling him to stop and come inside! We have played for just a short time, and because it is getting warmer, my mom decides to end our game until later. She gathers the toys from each of us and takes them back into the house.

I go lay down in the shade of the Catalpa tree. Now that spring is here, it has the huge leafs on it like Rosey told me. When a breeze comes up, it will blow the tiny white petals from the flowers down on the lawn like snow-flakes. And the grass with be covered in white. And yes, it is a great tree to cool off under. The other two have picked their spots to settle down also. Here comes my mom with her garden bucket that holds her tools. In her other hand, she's holding a couple of plastic six-pack pots with little plants in them. They will grow into larger flowers, like the ones in the flowerbeds. I love all the colors of the flowers in our yard. She digs the weeds out and plants the new pansies and snapdragons in and around the existing plants. There are lots of petunias in pots on the porch with the garden chairs, for when friends come to visit.

I love flowers as much as my mom does. She told me about a time when a friend came up onto the porch, and they remarked about how nice the yard looked. She told them,   "Yes,…. you too can have a park-like setting, even with Rottweilers."

At that time she had three of them. She said that she had to get after Ernie when he was a puppy, because those Terriers really love to dig, as that's part of who they are; digging for little mice and rats and rabbits.

With the days getting warmer and the pain medication Dr. Sara gave my mom, my shoulder and leg seem to be feeling better. So now we are going for longer walks. Oh how I love going to the park. One day at the park my mom was throwing a stick for me. I would race out and get it and bring it back to her. She would throw it again, and again. On the last throw, I ran after it hitting a wet spot in the grass. I went down sliding on my side. The one with the blister on my foot. Oh boy, did that hurt. I got up and limped back over to her.

"Quinn, what happened buddy?" she asked me looking very upset. I was kind of hot from running, so it looked like I was smiling at her. Deep down inside I wanted to cry. Rottweilers are very strong dogs, and usually don't cry. This was so painful, and we had to walk back through the huge parking lot, on past the baseball field, and up the street to our house. I got through the gate okay and down the driveway to the water-bucket for a drink. She let me in the house, where I limped straight down to my bed.

I could hear Ernie and Rosey outside running around, barking at people walking by the gate. I so wanted to go out and play with them, but my foot was swollen up bigger than I had ever seen it before.

My mom calls the other dogs for dinner. When she finishes feeding them, she comes in and fixes mine. That's when she calls me to come up and eat. It hurts to the point that I'm not sure if I can even get up. I lay there for a second or two, when I hear her call me again. "Quinn come, its dinnertime!"

No matter how much it is killing me, I want to do what she asks. So I pull myself up and limp over slowly to the stairs. Each step of my back foot sends a sharp pain through my leg. I see my mom looking my way, and I try to give her a little wag of my tail. One step at a time I slowly make my way over to my bowl. Even with the smell of chicken broth mixed in with good dog food, I'm just not hungry, so I turn and limp back down to my bed.

Stretching out on the soft flannel feels so comfy that I drift off to sleep. I am dreaming of running along with my pals, Ernie and Rosey, across a big field. Where there's tall, dried grass blowing in the wind. There are wild flowers of all sorts, in a wide blanket of purple and gold Lupine and Poppies outstretched as far as I can see. It's a sunny bright day, with puffs of clouds, in a almost clear blue sky. After racing back and forth, we come to a narrow creek-bed, where the water is rippling over piles of rocks. The three of us wade almost to the middle, and lap at the crystal clear water. It's very cold, as it comes from the run-off of the winter snow. I satisfy my thirst and find a soft spot in the grass to take a snooze. Rosey does the same as she is as worn out as I am. Now Ernie isn't one to do this sort of thing, being a Terrier and all. He goes off sniffing around, trying to catch the scent of a varmint or two. Funny little guy; he's always moving, and on the go.

I wake up to the sound of my mom coming down the stairs to check on me. It's time for my pain pill, as she opens my mouth wide and sticks all of her fingers with the pill down the back of my throat. I got to say, nobody has ever given me a pill of any kind, faster than this. I think she's had lots of practice with all those other Rottweilers.

She calls me to follow her upstairs to the living room, where I come and sit in front of her, and offer her my paw. I think that she likes it when I do this. My papa made it out to be the greatest thing he had ever seen a dog do. I liked doing that with him, 'cause that was all we could do together after we couldn't play ball any more. My other family treated me like I was an old guy, even when I still had lots of puppy-dog feelings left. This is why I love living with Ernie and Rosey. They seem to have fun everyday. Playing with the squeaky balls and chew toys. Even on the days I hurt, they still keep me going. As I sit here with my mom, she notices that my foot is swollen. She touches it, and I pull away in a great deal of pain. I look at her with big puppy dog eyes, letting her know that it hurts.

The next day starts off with my mom making another vet appointment for me. She is saying to the person on the phone that she noticed that my foot looks like it is swollen a little bit, and it needs to be looked at.

"Okay," she answers, "I'll have him there tomorrow morning."

"Gee, Quinn," Ernie says to me, "you haven't been here very long, and you've have more appointments with the vet than I think I've ever had."

"Ernie, stop picking on him. It's his leg or foot, or whatever." answers Rosey.

"Don't you think he wishes he was like us, where the only time he would go is for a check-up or a shot for something?"

"Well, Roe, I remember way back when I first came here, mom took me in to get me neutered." Ernie comments.

"Oh yeah," she replies, "I remember having to go get spayed. Boy was I sore for a while after that happened."

Ernie starts laughing, "Wow, I didn't think I was going to be able to walk again, let alone run anywhere."

The two of those guys just lay there laughing at some big joke I don't know anything about. I'm wondering, what can be so funny? Must have been a biggie if Ernie said that he was having trouble running! As serious as it sounds about going to the clinic and having whatever they had done, they didn't mention anything about doing any growling, or giving anyone trouble. And I've seen Ernie get ticked off at Rosey a few times, where he jumped at her growling, and meant it. He's got that Terrier attitude, where he's the tough guy. Then he turns around and is the nicest and funniest pup around. I go back to wondering about tomorrow and why I have to go back there again. I can't eat anything after midnight, because of what they have to do to me. And if I did I would get very sick.

It's morning and the other dogs are kenneled. My mom says that it's time to go. So I jump into the back of the car, and off we go, up and around, and down the street. I'm thinking, all I know is that I get to go for a ride in the car, and I'm certainly not worrying about this silly little bump between my two toes on my back foot. Again, it takes no time at all to get to the clinic. Once inside I am weighed and I have gained twenty pounds since the first time I came here back in February! That brightens up my mom some. I feel good when she is happy like that. Soon everything will be just fine, when I'm finally at the right weight for a Rottweiler.

My mom and I wait for someone to come and take me into the kennel room, where I will stay until they are ready for me. I heard Dr. Sommers is going to do a biopsy of the bump on my foot. That is where she will remove a piece of tissue that will be examined by a pathologist to see what's going on with this little bump. My mom has known Dr. Sommers for as long as she has known Dr. Sara, so my mom calls her by her first name, which is Katy. One of the nurses comes out to get me. But instead of taking me herself, she asks my mom if she would like to take me to the back where the kennels are. My mom smiles and says sure and walks back there with me. I like that a lot. She puts me in the kennel and says to me,

"Be good, Quinn, I'll be back later to get you."

I remember the first time she said that to me, about how she would be back later, and I didn't know what that meant. I smile and wiggle my tail at her, cause I know now that it's okay. That she'll be back for me, and I don't have to worry. I'm lying on the floor of the kennel, wondering when someone will come to get me. I hear the door open and footsteps coming towards where I am. I look up to see nurse Gina getting ready to take me into the big room. Now Dr. Sommers is instructing them to get me ready for sedation, and I remember what

Ernie and Rosey told me about being brave. I'm trying very hard to behave. They are not wasting anytime, or letting me try to control what's happening. Right off, they got me immobile with two people holding me still. But I start to growl anyway, getting pretty verbal. I wrestle around, trying to get loose, as they try to put the muzzle on. So I start shaking my head back and forth at the same time growling the deepest Rottweiler growl I can. They get the muzzle over my head and secure it, while I'm being firmly held still. Zap, goes the shot of tranquilizer,…. and I'm out.

Dr. Sommers doesn't like the way the bump looks, and proceeds to cut some tissue out, getting it ready to send off to be analyzed at the lab. She asks Denise to call my mom and asks, since I'm sedated, can they go ahead and neuter me? I guess my mom has talked to them about making an appointment to do this at another time. Not knowing that this other stuff was going to happen.

Later my mom calls to see how I'm doing. They tell her that the neutering was done, and that Katy didn't like what she saw with my toe. It looked like a tumor. I don't know what a tumor is, but from the long faces I see looking at me, it ain't good.

My friend Rosie, border collie/lab mix.

CHAPTER 9

THE CONE-SHAPED COLLAR

It's late in the afternoon when my mom shows up to take me home. I've been sleeping the whole time, and can't keep my eyes open. My eyelids are so very heavy. Denise talks to my mom, while she is waiting for someone to bring me out to the lobby. I feel so wobbly, like I'm a drunken sailor or something. I'm a mess as I'm being helped into the back of the car. Boy, I feel funny, and I have a suspicion that something has happened that I might not be too excited about later on down the road. But at the moment I don't care, I'll worry about it later. I have this goofy, big cone shaped collar around my neck. The purpose of this collar is to keep me from licking or chewing at the stitches from my surgery, which was me getting neutered. Humm. My foot is also wrapped with lots of bandages. *And* the pain medication is working quite well at this time.

My mom brings me into the house, where I am having the hardest time trying to get from one spot to another. I keep banging this silly cone of a collar into the doorways, walls and the sides of the porch rails. Slam! Whack! The collar warps out of shape as I hit something. I back away and the collar pops back into its rightful shape. Over and over this happens, and if not for the medication, I think I would become very annoyed. My mom realizes that this is not working with me.

She says to me, "Come on Quinn, let's kennel!" as she guides me down the front yard steps and leads me there.

"You can stay in here for a bit, while I go lay down for a nap. I don't feel too good right now."

She pets me on my back, and then turns and closes the kennel gate behind her. Ernie comes trotting over to the gate looking in at me. He starts to laugh and is yelling at Rosey to come see what happened to me.

"Hey Roe, guess what?" he shouts at her.

"It happened to the big guy." there is a huge smirk-like grin on his face.

"Ho, ho, ho," he just can't help teasing. Rosey comes running over across the lawn to the kennel, and just stares at me.

"Why are you guys acting this way?" I question them.

All the while I'm feeling like something just doesn't seem right. Even if I wanted to turn and look, this darn collar is not letting me do that. Rosey starts to slowly wag her tail at me, smiling as she says,

"You know the saying Quinn, it's for the best?"

"Yeah, I know that one, I've heard it a time or two, why?"

"Remember Ernie and me talking about getting spayed and neutered?"

"OH NOOO!!" I'm answering her as my mouth drops open. "Is THAT what happened to me, today?"

"Fraid so, Dude, you have just joined the "Neutered Dog Club of America! Where they say, Help control the pet population""

She gives me a sweet little grin, "Atta boy, Quinn," and turns and trots off, heading up to the porch, with Ernie following her, shaking his head, snickering the whole way. What a brat that guy is!

I've been in this kennel for just a little over an hour, and almost got this irritating collar off my neck. It's hanging like the big piece of plastic that it is, bumping into me every time I take a step. My foot is bugging me so that I've gotten most of that darn wrap off of it. I hear my mom's footsteps inside the house, coming down the stairs to the kennel door. The door opens and I can see her looking out. Once she gets her eyes focused on me, there is a look of shock on her face. I give her my biggest smile, and wiggle my tail so fast. I'm very glad to finally see her, and am anxious to show her what I've been doing since she left me here on my own.

"Hi mom, look what I did! I almost got this collar off me, aren't you proud of me?"

I want her know how hard a job it was, just to get it this far. And had there been more time before she opened the door, I would have had it completely off and would be able to see just what happened to me.

"Quinn" she gasps, "Oh, gads, what the heck happened?"

Her voice has nothing but panic in it. There are bloody paw prints all over the cement floor of the kennel. And she sees what a great job I was doing trying to take that darn collar off me.

"I should never have left you by yourself, I'm so sorry, buddy."

She comes over to me and starts undoing to rest of the string made out of gauge that has the cone tied to my collar,

"Hang on, I'll be right back."

She turns and runs through the doorway, hurrying up the stairs. I'm still standing there, thinking that I did a pretty good job getting this thing almost off me. Ernie hears all the commotion going on, and races down the porch stairs and over to the kennel gate. Looking through the wire, he just stares at what I've been doing.

"Oh, Dude, that isn't cool at all," as he is taken aback at the sight.

"Why is your foot all bloody, and what did they do to you besides getting neutered? When they neutered me nothing happened to my foot," he adds, staring at the mess I've made. He yells at Rosey to come see what's happened. She's up on the porch, looking down through the bench part of the railing. Holding her head down so she can see, she's frozen, as she takes in the sight of all this.

"Quinn, oh Quinn you poor guy." she whines at me.

"You look like you were in a battle of some sort."

With great urgency, she races down the stairs, she asks, "What happened?"

All I know is that cone-like collar was bugging me, and no matter what, I was going to get it off. And I tried to pull that darn wrap off my foot cause it felt too tight. I hear my mom running back down the stairs, flinging open the kennel door. She has some bandages in her hand.

"Quinn I have to fix this and take you back to the hospital. The answering service is going to have MAH call me back in a minute."

She no sooner gets the words out of her mouth when the phone rings.

"Hang on, I'll be right back."

It sounds like we have to go and have the vet see what I did to make my foot bleed so badly. My mom comes to get me into the car and off we go. She can't put the big cone-collar on me when I'm in the car, so she sets it on the passenger seat up front with her. We get to the clinic, and she helps me out. Inside the door, the receptionist, Jane looks at us, giving a little giggle to my mom. As she is paging a nurse to come to the lobby, she asks my mom, "What's going on?"

"I put him in the kennel, so I could lay down for a nap, and when I went to get him, his foot was unwrapped and blood all over everywhere."

She replied. "And to top it off, he had that dumb collar hanging half way off his neck."

Jane laughs jokingly, looking my way, "What are we going to do with you?"

I just stand there smiling and wagging my tail, cause here comes a treat being handed to me. Nurse Michael tells my mom that it would be fine to let me stay over night, so they can monitor my foot.

My mom gives me a hug and tells me to be good, and she will be back to get me tomorrow. I wag my tail at her, as I'm being lead back to the kennels. I see a friend of mine that I met before. She also is spending the night in the kennel next to me. So I feel okay about it, knowing that I won't be lonely tonight. I hear the door to the kennel room open, and see a lady that I don't know come and stop at my gate. She looks in at me, smiling.

"Let's get a look at your foot, Quinn." She says in a quiet voice.

She leads me out, and I follow her into the big room. She gets me to lie down and proceeds to take off the bandage that my mom hurriedly put on. She asks Kathy to bring some cleansing stuff to soak the dried blood off my foot, and she puts some salve on it, rewraps it nice and clean. After that she gives me some Chinese herbs to help stop the bleeding. I hear Kathy call the new lady Charlotte. She is also a veterinarian at my hospital. Her name is Dr. Burns. The only part I don't like is that they want to put that silly collar back on me. After this happens they take me back to my kennel, where there is a nice fluffy, clean blanket to lie on.

The dog next to me smiles at the sight of my collar. She sniffs at it through the wire of her kennel, saying how she didn't like it either when she had to wear one. She said that it was awkward, and got caught on everything. I told her how I tried and almost succeeded in getting it off. We both settle down to rest. I can't see her as easily as she can see me, because this collar is as far out as the end of my nose. It's okay to lay my head down with it on, because it flattens out. I feel pretty good right now, because I don't hurt anywhere.

The hospital is quieting down as it has been closed for a bit now. Someone comes into the kennel room, and gives me and the other dog some wet dog food. Because it has been a long day and is way pass my dinnertime, I am very hungry. I eat all of the food, and lick the bowl clean, finishing it off with a big drink of water. I'm just about ready to settle down, when someone comes to let me out, so I can take care of business before the night sets in. Then she brings me back to my kennel and gives me a big hug, petting me, and telling me I'm a good boy. I lie down and drift off to sleep, dreaming of my family, and how my life has changed.

In the morning the hospital comes alive with the hustle, bustle of another day. One of the nurses comes and takes me outside. After coming back in, I'm given my medication and breakfast. A staff person comes to get me and takes me into the big room, where Dr. LaRue wants to take a look at my foot. Then it is wrapped again and I'm back in the kennel, waiting for my mom to come get me to take me home. I'm getting to slowly meet all the employees at this hospital. I don't think I've ever known this many people in all of the eight years of my life. What I really like, is that they are all friends to me. Everyone seems to like me as much as I like them.

I've had some time now, to ponder what Ernie and Rosey told me about how I should behave when I'm here. So far, since I got here yesterday afternoon, no one has hurt me. No one stuck any needles in me at all. Humm, I was beginning to really think that's what happened when a dog came to the hospital, and the only way I knew how to cover up being a baby was to growl very loud at whoever was hurting me.

Man, I did growl pretty loud at Dr. Sara, and continued to try to even growl louder, when I thought she didn't hear me. And after all that, she still acts like she likes me. Ernie and Rosey told me that she has been their main veterinarian for a long time, along with Dr. Sommers and Dr. LaRue. Ernie used to go to them when they were in the old hospital on So. State St., so that's why he is so cool when he comes here to see them. Since Rosey was born after they opened this hospital, it's the only one she knows. I used to go to another clinic, before I started coming here, but not very often. This one is larger and newer than my other one.

The next day my mom brings me back so Dr. Sara can look at my foot. She is waiting to find out what the diagnosis is from the biopsy that Dr. Sommers did. Nurse Terry takes me out of the examination room, leaving my mom waiting there. She has to rewrap my foot again. Before my mom and I leave for home, nurse Terry gives her some medication for me, pain pills, and antibiotics. On the way home, we stop at Myers Pharmacy, and get some gauze and stretchy wrap, so she can change the bandages herself. They need to be changed every third day. I'm already going to the vets once a week. This is good, because with my mom changing the wrap, she can see for herself what's going on with my foot.

The next day is not a happy one for her, or me for that matter. Dr. Sara calls my mom to break the news about the results from the biopsy, and it's not good. I have what is known as a Mast Cell tumor. I hear Dr. Sara say that it's a form of cancer that is very unpredictable. It can be benign, which is harmless, or very nasty. If it is found in time they will do better with treatments. These tumors can spread quickly throughout the body. Chemotherapy is used to reduce the tumor, and chemo is very toxic. Then surgery is preformed to remove it. Dr. Sara wants me to have chemo, hoping that the tumor will shrink. Then she may have to perform surgery. She wants me to come in so she can check me over. My mom is so upset by this news; she wants to do whatever she can to make me better. I think it's harder on her than it is on me. For one thing, I don't know what is going to happen to me in the days ahead. But she has gone through this with her other Rottweilers, along with her own battle with breast cancer. She knows that it is going to be a tough fight.

We get to the clinic and go inside, where I get on the scale to be weighed. I have lost a couple of pounds because there were days that I didn't feel like eating. This also bothers my mom, as she would like to see me at least 100 pounds. Erin is at the desk, and sees me when I come in. She says, "Hi Quinn, how about a treat" as she is pulling one out of the jar on the counter. Michelle is another lady who works behind the desk. She gets up and comes to the swinging door. It's low enough that I can see over it easily. She too, reaches into the jar and pulls out a treat. I can't stop my tail from wagging at these ladies. I really am beginning to love them more and more. I'm also beginning to feel like this place is my second home. Ernie was right about me coming here more than he or Rosey.

My mom and I having one of our talks.

I'm with my friend, Ashley.

CHAPTER 10

My First Chemo Treatment

Nurse Terry takes me to change my bandages. Then she brings me back to the exam room, where my mom is waiting to talk to Dr. Sara. They are going to discuss how to deal with this tumor, depending on how bad it is. This might be why there's pain in my back leg, along with the pain in my front leg. Dr. Sara comes and checks me over, as she is telling my mom about the results of the biopsy. She wants to remove the tumor. I hear her tell my mom that she might have to remove a toe or two. My mom answers her by saying if that's so, take his leg. Wow! I sure hope that doesn't happen. She must not be thinking clearly. But I know she wants to do whatever it takes to make me well. Dr.Sara tells her, "He's going to need a chemo treatment tomorrow, so I want you to bring him in early and drop him off for the day."

My mom knows how long it takes for a person to have a chemo treatment, and because Dr. Sara told her to leave me for the day, she asks,

"Will he be hooked up to an IV for five or more hours like I was?"

"No, no, no!" Sara reassures her. "We just put a catheter in with the chemo. And that's that."

She tells my mom that because I need to start my chemo treatments right away and don't have an appointment, I need to be dropped off and kenneled until they can find the time to work me in.

"Okay, Sara we will be here, bright and early." She nods as we turn and head for the door.

I'm only eight-years-old, and my mom knows that I have a couple more years left in me. She says I act like I'm six.

The next day it's a marvelous morning, and instead of spending it with my buddies, I get to go have a chemo treatment, whatever that is. On the way out to the car, my mom explains to me that I'm lucky that I won't have to be hooked up all day, like she was. And that Denise told her I wouldn't be losing my hair. I guess that's what happened to my mom when she had her treatments.

I follow her out to the car. When she opens the door, she says,

"Load up, Quinn, want to go see Sara?"

I wag my tail and hop into the back and lay down for the quick trip to the vets. I love getting to go see Dr. Sara, as we are becoming good friends. Coming in through the door, I notice a different receptionist, whose name is April. As she sees my mom and me, she pulls out my chart.

"Hey Quinn, how's it going?" she asks me. "I have a treat for you."

I wag my tail at her, and give a big smile. These guys are turning out to be really good friends of mine. And someone is always petting me, and telling me that I'm a good boy. Sometimes there are other dogs waiting in the lobby at the same time I am. I don't notice them getting any treats like I get. Maybe they got theirs already before I came in.

Here comes that guy, Danny from the back, out into the lobby. He is walking towards my mom and me. He smiles at us, as he says,

"Come on big guy, you're coming with me."

All I do is wag my tail and trot down the hallway away from my mom. I know now that when I come back out, no matter what time it is, she will be waiting for me.

Dr. Sara sees me and smiles, as Danny is slipping the muzzle over my head. She is getting things prepared for what she has to do. Danny asks Gina to give him a hand at lifting me up onto the table. I'm thinking, "Here we go again." I feel very uncomfortable up here, just because I'm on this table, if for no other reason than that. Thoughts of what Ernie and Rosey told me are racing through my head, and I really want to be good. Danny has me in what's called a head-lock, where his arm is over my shoulder, leaning on me with his head pressed next to mine like we're hugging. Gina has my front leg straightened out and is pushing the catheter in where she shaved my leg. At the same time I'm trying my hardest to pull away. I think of Ernie letting them do this to him, and he doesn't get mad. Makes me wonder, why do I have to try to be so tough?

Everything is a repeat of the first time I came into the big room for x-rays. And like the first time, I don't want any part of it. How come they have to put me through this and why is this happening?

I've got to try and scare them more than they are scaring me. I let out the biggest growl ever! One would almost think I was a grizzly bear with the volume of noise I'm making. I now raise my growling a notch or two, trying to convince them to let me be. As Gina is trying to finish doing her part, I see Dr. Sara standing behind her. She and everybody else in the room know that I'm not happy with what's going on. To make my point clearer, I growl a little deeper and louder. As I'm growling in a menacing grumble to warn them to back off. Dr. Sara steps in front of Gina. She places her hands on both sides of my ears, pressing them firmly to my head, so I can't move it back and forth anymore, or even try to get away from her. As her eyes are staring deep into mine, practically right through me, I'm still trying to let her know I'm not going for any of this. Then for one split second our eyes lock together, and she softly but with strict authority says, *"You've got to trust me! You've got to trust me! You've got to trust me!"*

I have been so tense, trying to fight off this power struggle. Oh, I don't want to growl like I've been doing to her. She is my very good friend, but I am so scared right now. Then with a deafening BAM-KABOOM! something claps loudly in my brain; all the thoughts and things that were said to me. In an instant they come crashing together, and start to click in. Wow, it all makes sense. I flash back to what Lillie said about how Dr. Sara and the other veterinarians are here to make us better. Ernie, Rosey and my mom kept telling me over and over to be a big boy and let them do what they have to do to make me well. Right now I don't know this, but I am a very sick boy. Somehow it is all beginning to make sense, and I totally relax, letting out a big sigh. The realization of what is happening is over-whelming. I'm thinking, why did I put everybody though this, as I settle back and let them do what they were trying to do all along, which was to make me better. It is at this moment that I "bite the bullet" like Ernie told me to do, and let Danny sedate me. I am very lucky that Dr. Sara didn't give up on me either.

It has been a long time since they put me in one of the kennels to sleep off the anesthetic. I'm so messed up. Dr. Sara had to do x-rays and aspirate one of my lymph nodes, which means removing the fluids. I feel sick to my stomach, and no way want anything to eat plus, standing up is not an option at this time. I try but my legs just aren't co-operating with me. So I settle down, and slide back to dreaming of being safely back with my family. I don't remember the ride home, and I'm guessing that I went straight to my blanket, only to wake up when my mom comes down to take me outside to get me ready for bed.

Next morning is a great day, and I'm up and out in the yard with my buddies, sniffing all around the bushes. I even trot over to the fence and start to peek through the gap to see if I can see Dakota. I'm about to stick my nose up close to the fence, when I'm set back by the biggest, if not loudest blasting bark I have ever heard.

"WOOF WOOF WOOF! Back off!!"

I jerk my head as I almost jump out of my fur away from the shaking fence. I didn't know it, but he was crouched right there, laying in wait in the most wolf-like way.

"Gees Dakota, I just want to be friends with you, come on!"

I say to him trying to be nice. He grumbles back at me, something about being part of Ernie's family, and that Ernie has been taunting him for years through the fence.

"Yeah, but I'm not Ernie, I'm Quinn and I like everybody, including you. Can't we be friends?"

Ernie hears what's going on and races over to the fence. He slams into it, and has his teeth bared, all the while jumping on the fence. It's then that my mom comes running out and starts yelling at Ernie to stop that barking right now. But Ernie being Ernie, he has to have the last word before he turns and trots back over to the porch and up the stairs. At the same time, he's grinning like he showed Dakota a thing or two. My mom comes out with our toys, and we all have a go at playing with her. Boy, I sure feel a lot better than I have been. They've given me some new pain medication, and it's really working. All of a sudden, Ernie breaks off from playing with his squeaky toy and races as fast as he can towards the gate. Rosey is right behind him, as people are walking by with their dogs. Then as always, they turn on each other. I also stop playing and trot up to the gate to watch what is going on. I still can't understand the carrying on they do. There is barking going on behind me. I look over my shoulder to see Ginger, the pretty dog next door. She looks like she's a Chow-Shepherd mix and has a rusty-red coat that is very thick. She's about the same size as Rosey.

"Hi Ginger." I smile and wag my stubby tail at her.

She's just standing there looking kind of funny at me. I get close to the wire fence and stick my nose through it and touch hers. It's then that she asks me,

"What's up with your leg, Quinn? It looks like it's swollen a little," as she's staring at it.

"Oh, I don't know, I got a bump between my middle toes, and my leg hurts, so I had to go see my veterinarian about this."

I continued to tell her about how they did some tests, and that it looked like I might have a Mast Cell tumor. She said that she was friends with Mae, the Rottweiler that was here when she came to live next door. I was in no-way ready to hear what was going to be told to me next. Apparently my mom found a bump on Mae's foot just like the one on mine. She took Mae to the vets, to have it looked at. It turned out to be a Mast Cell tumor, and they removed it and one of her toes.

"Oooh really, did I hear you say....removed?" I questioned her. And at the same time I get a flash-back of the conversation between my mom and Dr. Sara, when they first talked about how to handle this bump.

"Yep, and she was okay for a little while after that." Ginger replied. "That Mae always had her little tail just a wagging all the time. I remember every time your mom would call her or say her name, that tail would start moving as fast as it could."

"Then what happened?" I asked.

Ginger went on to say, that Mae would always go out and get the paper in the morning and bring it back to my mom. And when Rosey was a pup she saw what Mae did, and started grabbing the paper away from her. And in doing so, it always got ripped. So Mae stopped getting the paper, because she didn't like the way your mom got mad at a ripped paper all the time. And besides Rosey was so much faster than Mae was, she got to the paper before Mae was even off the front porch.

"My mom told me some neat stuff about Mae." I said to Ginger.

How she and my mom drove to Eureka one day to bring a friend back to Ukiah, and that they just hung out all day walking around killing time until the friend met up with them. They had a very tight bond going on between them.

Ginger went on to tell me about a dog walk the Humane Society had, where they walked from the City Park down to Dora St., and then on to Alex Thomas Plaza, which was down on School St. It was a very long walk. Ernie was with Ashley, and when they got to Standley St., Ashley and Ernie went on with a friend while my mom and Mae headed back up to the Park. She said that Mae had told her all about it when she got home, and Mae was so glad her mom had turned around to go back. She was getting older when that happened.

Mae told Ginger that she and my mom used to have "talks" after they were in for the night. Mae would sit in front of her, while she got a massage and her ears scratched. She was ten years old and slowing down some. The vet, who wasn't my Dr. Sara, was trying different medications. Mae had her appointment on Friday. Over the week-end she just laid around, not feeling good at all. She was very much like me, in the way she would get up and go downstairs to her bed when she wasn't feeling good. Sunday evening after her one-on-one time with my mom, Mae got up and instead of going downstairs, she went over to one of her favorite spots next to the wooden chest by the stairs that led to the upstairs bedroom. As she lay there, she had her eyes on my mom, like she was trying to communicate, and it didn't take but a moment or two until my mom looked over at Mae. Quietly she took her time looking back, without breaking the stare going on between them. After what seemed like an eternity my mom said,

"Okay girl, I guess you know better than anyone, when the time is right."

So the next day an appointment was made to bring Mae in around six in the evening. In the afternoon, Ernie, Rosey and Mae had her going away party. It meant that they would get left-over roast and veggies in with their kibble, and topped off with each one getting a Frosty Paws ice cream.

By now Ernie has come away from the gate, and is sitting next to me listening to this story that Ginger is telling me. He interrupts Ginger asking her if she knew the rest of the story.

"Well, no I never heard what happened after Mae left to go to the vets." She replied. "I do know that I never saw her again!"

So Ernie continued to finish telling me about what happened. On the way to the clinic my mom stopped by "Town & Country Grooming", so Mae's friend Robin, the groomer could say good-bye. Robin was a big part in Mae's life. She was the person who got Mae's mom and dad together for a breeding. Her grand-pa on her dad's side was a Champion titled Rottweiler, from back in the 80's. He was a very sought after gentleman.

My mom and Mae were waiting in the "Quiet room" at the vets, when the door flew open and the new vet rushed in saying,

"What happened over the week-end?" in an annoying manner.

All she had done on Friday was cut Mae's meds in half. She wanted to know what was going on, and why my mom was there to put Mae down. After telling the vet that she knew her dogs better than anybody and that it was time, the vet did what she was expected to do. But it left a huge question mark in my mom's head as she slowly drove out of the parking lot, crying and very confused about what had just happened, questioning herself and wondering all the way home if she had just cut Mae's life shorter than it should've been. Ernie said that when my mom got home from the vets and was very upset, and crying. He followed her into the house, where she just sat on the stair by Mae's spot, staring over towards the window. Finally she picked up the phone to talk to a friend, wanting to talk to someone about the horrible ordeal she had just been through She felt that maybe she'd made the wrong decision. All the while in her heart, she knew that it was Mae's decision that mattered. She was still confused by what had happened, when a couple of days later the phone rang, and it was Dr. Rice.

"Oh, hi Sara, what's up?" my mom asked.

Sara asked her about Mae. My mom got upset all over again about the way things happened with the other vet. She was confused as to whether she had done the right thing or not. Dr. Rice told her that she was not there that day, but when she came in, she pulled the charts to see what had gone on. When she read Mae's chart, she knew that the time had been right, and that my mom *had* done the right thing, in respecting Mae's decision, and to be thankful for the wonderful communication that had gone on between the two of them. Ginger was sitting there listening as Ernie finished telling the story. She looked at me, and said. "Boy, your mom really loves her dogs; you are a lucky guy to have found her."

I smiled and wiggled my stubby tail at her, and replied, "Yes, you're right about me being lucky, but she's the one that found me!"

Then she told me about the other Rottweiler that was here before me. The one named Jazz, who she said had arthritis. It was so bad, that every time she went outside, her rear-end would go out from under her. She went on to say that my mom took a towel and made it into a sling to help Jazz stand up, when she was out to take care of business. And how Jazz would have no part of that. She was much too proud. But this big girl hadn't been with her new family very long to learn that when my mom came home from a chemo treatment and wasn't feeling well at all, she would lay by her feet, while Ernie and Rosey kept running in and out of the house. She seemed to know that this was where she was supposed to be. Your mom gave her lots of love in return. Jazz had lived here almost a year, when one day her rear-end just kept going out on her. She had to be helped up about ten times in one hour. She looked so sad at your mom, that was the moment it was decided to make the call to the vets, to bring her in. Dr. Sommers was running her hand over Jazz's spine, when she asked what the problem was. "Severe arthritis!"

"Oh, no she has a slipped disk." Said Dr. Sommers. So the end for Jazz had come. The last year of her life she was covered with respect and love. She in turn got to be the companion dog she longed to be. She was missed very much.

"Yeah, I heard about her from those two," who are now back up at the gate barking at more people walking by.

"You Rottweilers have a lot of health problems going on with you, huh?"

"I don't know, I've never been sick before."

Ginger went on to tell me that she had been a shelter dog at one time. And her person named Becky, adopted her. She is a lot like me, as far as liking all the dogs she meets. She said she has gotten along with every dog that has lived here.

One thing that surprised me was that she also liked Lillie, and didn't mind when she came over into her yard to hunt. She said that Lillie would hide in the flowers for very long periods of time, waiting for an alligator lizard to come out from under a rock. Then she would grab it, and take off running through the wire fence towards the house with it hanging out of her mouth. Ginger wasn't sure what Lillie did with it, but knowing that cat like I've learned to, she headed straight into the house to show it off to my mom.

Lillie Billie Boop Bop aka Lillie

One of my favorite things is shaking hands.

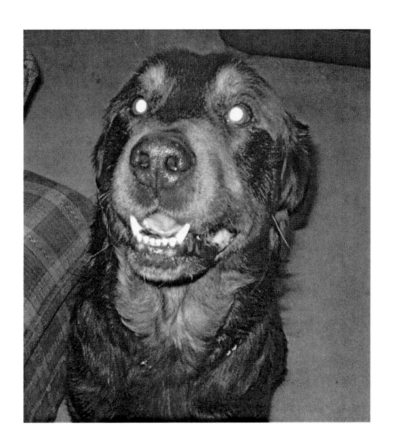

Me, before I got sick

After the tumor was removed

CHAPTER 11

THE E-MAILS START

Dr. Sara wants my mom to email her everyday to see how I am doing. This is because Dr. Sara is not only a veterinarian, she is also very interested in veterinary oncology. This is where she treats dogs that get cancer of some sort or another. So now I am under her care receiving chemo treatments, and different medications to help me get through this. Plus, natural herbs, along with anything that she learns about, by going to seminars. She is constantly talking to different veterinarians about new studies that are happening. She, along with my mom wants me to get well and be a healthy boy again. There will be emails to her about how I'm doing everyday. On the afternoon I came home from being sedated to have x-rays done and the lymph node aspirated, my mom emailed Dr. Sara.

The email said,

"Quinn was a mess Fri night. He had a blank look in his eyes. Was not with it at all. Sat morning he is back to normal. Is eating fine."

On Saturday I was feeling so good, that we went to dog class. I love seeing my friends there. And going through the obedience lessons with my mom. Oh man let me say that there are treats of all kinds at class. Charlee Bear treats with cheese and egg, and pieces of turkey, cheese, hot dogs. And every time I do well, my mom makes sure I get my treat. I'm beginning to feel pretty good now.

Gee, a whole week has gone by without me having to go to see Dr. Sara. I've been playing with my pals, going for car rides to the store, walks to the City Park to watch the little kids playing on the swings and sliding down the slides as they giggle and scream among themselves. All under the watchful eye of their moms or dads. I have been as happy as I would ever want to be. My medication is doing just fine. Today I'm off to see Dr. Sara for blood work and a chemo treatment. This is kind of like when my mom was getting her treatments. She would go to the hospital lab and have them take blood, so her oncologist would know what her blood count was. And the next day she would go for a chemo treatment. Most of the days she would have to bring a lunch, because she would be there all day long. My treatments, thank goodness, aren't like that.

Danny comes out to the lobby where my mom and I are waiting. As he takes my leash, he has a big grin on his face. He says to her,

"I can't believe this is the same dog! Don't know what you've been doing with him, but he's turned completely around and doesn't give me trouble anymore."

My mom replies laughing, "It was Sara getting in his face that did it."

All of that is true I'm thinking as I hear this. They don't know about my conversations with Ernie and Rosey. Even Lillie set me straight on how to behave at the vets. And because of this, something feels better with me as I follow him into the big room. I can't believe that I'm letting them put me up on the table without giving them any trouble. It doesn't make any difference anymore. And I can tell that they are very pleased with the way I am acting. Today there's a lot happening with me, and Dr. Sara wants me to be sedated. This is okay with me, and from now on I will behave and act like a good Rottweiler should. It always was scary, before the big *awakening* happened to me. From now on I will make my mom and Dr. Sara proud of the way I've changed into the best dog ever. I'm glad they didn't give up on me. Because of this, I also helped Dr. Sara understand big black dogs better.

Things are going so well, that one night when my mom is on the computer looking at her mail, she sees one from Dr. Sara that says.

"RE: The Deal and she opens it. Dr. Sara is a little bit disturbed with her and wrote:

"The deal is that you email me and let me know how he is doing" ...S.

My mom looks at me with a sheepist grin on her face, and says, "Huh oh, Sara's not happy with me, Quinn."

She answers by apologizing for slipping, but that I'm doing so good that she thinks it's not necessary to say anything at the time. Sometimes my mom's way of thinking is, if it ain't broke, don't try to fix it. That means if everything is cool, let it be. Now on the other hand Dr. Sara is doing an on going study of her cancer patients, and *wants* to know when I'm feeling good or bad, no matter what. Later on down the road, it hits my mom that it makes sense why Dr. Sara needs to know one way or another. This is a way for doctors to find out about different reactions to treatments or medications. Also if there are any side effects.

It was a big deal the day that Dr. Sara asked me to trust her, and the start of our emotional tie to each other. My mom told me that she had never seen this happen between her dogs and their vet before, and that Dr. Rice was respected by all of her pets.

Saturday I was feeling so good after my chemo treatment the day before that my mom took me to dog class and I had a great time seeing my friends there, and learning how to be a good boy at all times. It's Sunday now and I've just come in from out in the yard with Ernie. I love that old guy; he is so full of mischief and trying to be funny all at the same time. The only time I've seen him serious is when it starts to get close to dinnertime. Rosey has been lying by my mom snoozing. She is a high-energy dog that would probably like other jobs besides just getting the paper in the morning and running hard after the ball. When she's in the house, she is very laid-back and likes to take naps.

I go to see what my mom is doing. She is on that computer thing, sending an email to Dr. Sara; telling her how good I feel. She says,

"Quinn is just his old-self. Following the other two around, running up to the gate, etc. If I didn't know the facts, I would say this dog is in perfect condition...mt

I have a follow-up appointment with Dr. Sara today. We get to the clinic, and nurse Terry calls us into the exam room. I'm not aware my mom's friend Denise and nurse Terry are competing to see who is going to give me the better treat. All I can do is wiggle my stubby little tail as fast as it will go whenever I see either one of them. I don't know which is better, them giving me a treat or the girls behind the receptionist desk in the lobby.

We are waiting for Dr. Sara to come and see me. There is something that my mom is concerned about. When she was brushing me yesterday, she noticed on one side of me that my black fur had a white mark there. She brushed my coat in the opposite direction and could see that it was about a foot long and only about two inches wide. It looked like I had rubbed against a newly painted fence slat. When Dr. Sara came in, she had her big smile on, as she asked how things were going. My mom started laughing, as she showed Dr. Sara my 'paint' mark on my side. I don't think she has ever seen anything like this before. My mom says to her,

"Do you think it's from the chemo treatment?"

Dr. Sara answers, "I'm not sure, we'll just keep an eye on this, and see what happens."

Things have been getting a little exciting around here. My mom has some really good friends that moved to Hawaii a couple of years ago. They still have family over here in California. His name is Robbie, and his grand-daughter is the same age as my mom's oldest grand-daughter, Ashley. And they are both graduating from middle school. They live in different towns, so will go to different high schools. Robbie is coming over and staying at our house, because they have been best friends for many, many years. They want to use the time to visit for a day or two, before he goes to his family and the graduation that will be taking place in Lake County.

My mom says that I will like Robbie. But I already know this, cause like I've said many times before; I like everybody that I meet. She puts us in our kennel and drives down to the Santa Rosa airport to pick up Robbie and bring him back to our house. I can't wait to meet this person, as he is a dog-lover. Years ago he took one of my mom's Rottweilers to work with him everyday, when he worked in the construction business. Her name was Maja and she loved doing things with him. She was one of the first two Rottweilers that started my mom on her love affair with my breed, and she was a very serious girl. My mom told me about when they would be riding in the car, and my mom would be driving and talking to a friend at the same time, not looking at the road. Maja would stick her head between the front seats and stare at her, saying, "Better keep your eyes on the road, or I will have to take the wheel and drive for you!"

Another time my mom got pulled over by the Highway Patrol, the officer said she was speeding.

"But I was in the middle lane and people were passing me."

"Well, you swerved back there." He replied.

Maja was sitting on the passengers' seat while this was going on. Seeing that my mom was getting annoyed at the cop telling her she was speeding and then changing it to her swerving, Maja leaned quickly over across the front of her and filled the whole open window, staring at the cop. All the while having a look on her face that said,

"Listen, officer we have places to go, and people to see, and you are holding us up!"

When the cop saw Maja was a big Rottweiler, he took one giant step back, glaring at both of them, and telling her to watch her driving. According to my mom, Maja was a no nonsense kind of girl. I love it when I sit in front of my mom, shaking her hand as she tells me stories about the Rottweilers she had before me. She gave them all lots of love and a wonderful home.

It is around midnight when I hear the car pull into the carport. My mom and Robbie are up and onto the porch, as I get a glimpse of them before they go inside and turn the lights on. She tells Robbie where to put his bag and packages, before she comes to let us out of the kennel. Ernie says,

"Come on, Quinn you gotta meet this guy, he's one of my friends."

Ernie knocks Rosey and me out of his way getting through the kennel gate, racing up the stairs before we are even across the lawn.

As Robbie sees Ernie, he says with a big smile,

"Hey, Ernesto buddy, how's it going,"

Giving Ernie loving scratches behind his ears, as Ernie is jumping up on him. My mom sternly says to Ernie,

"Off, Ernie, stop jumping on Robbie!"

Robbie says hello to Rosey as he pets her and gives her a hug. Then he turns to me and says,

"Nice looking guy, he kind of looks like a 'Mortie', kind of dog!" and pets me on the head. My mom tells him to shake my paw, as she says. "Cause Quinn loves to shake hands with everybody."

I'm sitting in front of him, offering him my paw and giving him my big Rottie smile that I'm so famous for....

There's a lot of hustle, bustle going on around the house. I'm not sure what it's about, because my days this last couple of weeks have been in and out of the clinic. Anything outside of that I've forgotten about. Rosey reminds me,

"Today is Ashley graduation, don't you remember?"

"Oh, that's right, duh, that's why Robbie is here!"

I laugh back at her. My mom and Robbie are getting ready to go up to Willits to see Ashley's graduation from middle school into high school. My mom is very proud of her oldest grand-daughter. The graduation is scheduled to start at 6:00 pm. It is almost time for Robbie and my mom to leave. We are out in the yard running around waiting to be put in the kennel. I hear her coming down the stairs and open the back door, calling to us to come and kennel. We hurry through the gate, as she closes it. Rosey jumps up onto the doghouse to lie down. Ernie and I sit in front of the gate and watch as Robbie and my mom leave. It will be late when they get back.

CHAPTER 12

REMOVING THE TUMOR

I don't know this now, but today is the day I go back to the vets. Dr. Sara will be removing the tumor, and maybe a toe or two along with it. She wants to make sure that there will be no cancer left. My mom gets me into the car for my ride to the clinic, for what she thinks is another chemo treatment. With Ashley's graduation and Robbie coming to stay a few days before he goes over to Lake Co, she has forgotten it's time for my operation.

The girls at the desk must have known that I'm here to have my tumor removed, because there are no treats today, they just smile and say,

"Hi Quinn, What a good boy you are!"

As they pat me on my head, I smile and wag my tail at my mom one more time before I'm lead down the hallway to the kennels. The gate is already open, so I trot on in and turn around and sit staring towards the big room. I start to daydream about what is going to happen to me today. My mom and Dr. Sara try to hide what they're feeling behind smiling faces when they are around me. I smile back with my wiggly tail moving ever so fast. And for one spilt second I see a flash of sadness in their eyes. We look back at each other, and that's when the trust and love deepens, for it is at these times I know Dr. Sara is doing everything she can to make me well, and rid my body from this ugly monster that is trying to take over. And from seeing my mom at times, I know that she is so upset that this happened to me. And so sad, praying that a miracle will happen. She's also very angry, knowing that my time will be cut way too short.

After talking to Rosey and especially Ernie cause he's been around the longest I'm beginning to figure out that I'm sicker than anybody wants to talk about. At first my mom and Dr. Sara would talk back and forth in front of me. I would hear what they were saying, but at that time I didn't know what they were talking about. I notice, as I'm led back out to the lobby, my mom and Dr. Sara stop talking when they see me coming towards them. I guess they don't want me to hear how bad it is. But Dr. Sara is always optimistic about my treatments doing the job to make me well again.

On the other hand my mom sees how I look and act when I get home from a treatment. That really upsets her, and it hurts her when she sees me heading to go downstairs to my blanket, not even looking back her way, so she knows that I don't feel very good. Then she is very happy the next day if I'm up and running the gate with my pals, or teasing Dakota. Even though she disapproves of that behavior, she knows when I'm doing this stuff, I feel good. Every once in a while my shoulder and front leg really hurt me, when I'm running around crazy-like with Ernie. That's when I start limping, and don't want my mom to see me doing that. So I kind of throw in a little spring to my step, and hope that I can hide it from her.

It's later in the afternoon, and I am coming out of the anesthetic. I'm very groggy and don't really feel anything. I'm in a fog as to where I am. Things begin to clear a little as I hear Denise telling me that they want to keep me here for the night.

CHAPTER 13

Our Camping Trip

Thursday, June 12, Dr. Sara sends an email saying, *"He was a trooper and let Denise put in a catheter without any grumble--you are doing such a great job with him!! Surgery was long and tough and he lost just one toe, but hopefully he lost a lot more--like the cancer nodule. It will be at first an irritated area (like with the biopsy) but hopefully will be gone once we are 10-14 days post op. I am hoping for the very best outcome for him and for you--he is quite wonderful. S*

My mom is sitting there at the computer reading this, thinking about the way I'm acting. And she answers,

"He is sooo out of it. Just lays there and pees on himself. I tried to get him up to go outside (did once) but he justs lays there. He did take a bisquit this evening, but just lay back down. See ya tomorrow.." mt

The peeing is from the Prednisone, and as it tapers off, that will stop. I can't help it, so my mom is confining me to the kitchen. She's put layers of newspaper down all over the floor, and I'm staying behind the kiddie-gate, so I can't make a mess by lying around any place I want. My mom takes good care of me, and wants me to be comfortable while I'm going through all this. If this was happening at my other house, I would be out in the shed. And probably wetting my rug or blanket, and nobody even knowing that was happening. This shows how very much I'm being loved and cared for. I'll be okay, and close by so she can keep an eye on me.

We are back at the clinic for a follow-up, and Dr. Sara is shown my other side, where there's yet another thin, long, white, paint-like stripe going from my shoulder half-way down my side. Again Dr. Sara is not sure what the cause is.

I'm very excited today, because Ernie and Rosey just got through telling me about a dog that is coming to stay with us. It's not Annie, but another girl that's the same age as Rosey. Her name is Sophie, and my mom's friend, Chris got her from the City Animal Shelter. Chris' wife had to put her beloved Mickey down. He was an old guy, and the time had come to do the right thing, which was to let him go to the "Rainbow Bridge".

I've heard that the Rainbow Bridge is where dogs and other pets go after they leave their earthly bodies. And there is no more pain and suffering among them. It's there they can run with friends old and new. The old and sick are made young and well again. And ones who were injured become healed and healthy. Nobody needs food or water, because that's not necessary there. The days go by with lots of playing and chasing going on. But there will be a day when your dog will stop in his tracks, as he sees, off in the distance, someone familiar to him. Realizing it's you, he will take off running as fast as he can to you! And after all the hugs and kisses are exchanged, the two of you will then cross the Rainbow Bridge together. Even though this is the way it ends, none of us dogs here know about this for sure. We don't think about these things. After all, we live in the here and now to have fun with and please our human friends.

It's in the middle of the day, around lunchtime that my mom tells us to go to the kennel. Sophie will be here very soon. She's a little bit shyer than Annie, and if we greeted her at the gate like we do Annie, she would probably pee all over herself. Besides being shy, she is very careful of the way she acts around people outside of her family. My mom told me she likes Sophie when she comes here, because she's always good and behaves nicely. Rosey and Sophie are the same size, age, and color, medium black dog with a little bit of white. They look like they could've come from the same litter. Sophie's hair is shorter and straighter than Rosey's, and she looks like a pointer, while Rosey looks like a bigger Border collie. There might be a little bit of Labrador Retriever mixed in there with her. Rosey's dad was a black Lab, but my mom thinks she looks more like a Flat-coated Retriever, because her fur is wavy instead of straight. We hear a noise coming down the driveway, as Sophie is flying up onto the porch and skids to a stop at the rail.

She looks down through the openings of the porch bench to where we are, for a second, then charges down the steps and over to the kennel gate. She's sniffing through the wire, and as her nose touches mine, she jerks back and stares at me.

"Hey who are you" she asks me.

"My dad said that MT had a new dog, but he didn't say that you were this handsome."

I feel a very warm feeling come over my face, and I can't help myself from a silly grin coming on. The gate is opened and Ernie pushes pass us to get to Sophie first, as Rosey and I bump into each other trying to make it out of the kennel. The four of us take off running all over the lawn playing tag. Chris and my mom are standing upon the porch looking out over the yard at us playing. Chris says,

"Looks like they're having a good time."

"Oh yeah, always." my mom answers.

This is good because next week is when Sophie will be staying for a whole week here. As my mom and Chris enjoy a visit with each other, we continue to play with Sophie. She doesn't see many other dogs, so she is really having a great time. An hour has passed, when Chris comes out to let Sophie know that it's time to go. I like Sophie, just like all my other friends. I can't believe all of the friends I've made in the four short months that I have lived with my new family. Even Lillie and I are now best friends. Sometimes I'm in the house and she is the only other one here. She's not one of many words, because most of the time she is snoozing. Boy do cats like to nap, and nap some more. She sometimes will stay in her spot up on the back of the couch all day long. After it gets dark she acts like it might be a night for a full moon. She goes racing out her door; and in a flash she's back in the house and flying toward the top of the counter by the front door. One night she knocked a planter off of there. The pot went crashing to the floor, throwing dirt and parts of the plant all over. And she was out her kitty-door quicker than a wink of your eye. Cats sure are hard to figure out.

In the morning she will bug my mom until she gets her half can of Fancy Feast cat food and her tummy is full. In her contented state she will then go out and take a nap in the sun on the porch, or head straight for the couch, where that nap will last for a long time. Then it won't be until late afternoon that she starts getting frisky and starts clawing the side of the couch, or jumping out at Rosey or even me. She doesn't bother Ernie so much, because if she makes a quick move towards him, he starts to snap at her. He catches himself right in the middle of it, and pulls back. That's because it's his way of controlling his prey drive. And he knows that he would be in big trouble if he did any harm to Lillie. Heck, he was the one that made all the racket when Jazz had gotten Lillie. And by doing that, my mom came out and scooped Lillie up and off to the vets right away. It was good that old Jazz didn't have sharp teeth anymore; they were worn down almost to her gums. That's what probably saved Lillie. Jazz could only bite just so hard. If she had been a younger dog or her teeth were sharper, she would have punctured a lung or something.

Ernie said to me, "It's a good thing that I started howling like I did. I think that's what made Jazz let go and drop her like a hot potato. She wasn't sure of what was going to happen when mom came running out." Lillie knows that Ernie would never hurt her. She respects him for being in control of his prey drive when he's around her. She also knows now that I would never harm her.

It's a good thing that Ernie has to be in the middle of everything. Like sounding the alarm when Jazz had Lillie's head in her mouth. He told me about the time that Morton II was having an aneurysm and my mom heard this high pitched yelping coming from the outside. It sounded like Ernie when he's screaming at the sound of the sirens on the fire trucks. My mom ran to the door and pushed it open, in time to see Ernie standing at the door, smiling at her. While over by the middle of the deck is Morton II laying there. His eyes wide open, and his tongue hanging out. Looking like he had just ran 10 miles.

Today Dr. Sara wants me to come to the clinic, so she can take a look at my foot and see how it's coming along. A couple of days ago, Denise had shown my mom how to wrap my foot. And it's a good thing cause we would have to come in every other day to get it changed. Denise sees me and hurries into the exam room where we are waiting for Dr. Sara. She has one of those really special cookies that has a paw print on it. They taste really delicious; I think they're made with peanut butter. She no sooner goes out one door than auntie Terry comes in the other. She also has a really good treat. Now I can't tell which one is better, Denise's or auntie Terry's, but I'm enjoying all of the attention I'm getting. (One day the phone rang and my mom answered it saying, "hello". The person on the other end said that she was my auntie Terry, calling from the animal hospital, when it was really nurse Terry calling my mom. So from then on I call her, auntie Terry.) She takes the wrap off my foot, and just as she finishes unwrapping it, Dr. Sara enters the room.

"THAT looks ugly!" gasps my mom, wrinkling up her nose.

"Ugly to some, beautiful to others, all in the way you look at it." answers Dr. Sara, grinning as she adds,

"It looks so good, I'm really happy with how it turned out."

Auntie Terry takes me into the big room to rewrap my foot, while Dr. Sara talks to my mom. She wants me to come back on Monday for a chemo treatment. Now that the tumor is removed, she wants to be aggressive in making sure that the bad cancer cells are killed.

The next day is dog class day, and I'm feeling pretty good, as I've been happily trotting all over the yard and up and down the driveway playing with my pals. We get to the class and my back foot has the wrap on it. All the other dogs in the class have been been asking me about it and want to know why is it wrapped? Since everybody is curious, Sandy tells the class that I had a cancerous tumor removed, but I feel fine enough to do my training. I'm standing there wagging my tail, feeling like the proud Rottweiler I should be. They don't have to know about the trouble I gave Dr. Sara at the clinic. She so wanted me to trust her, while the whole time I was worrying about them hurting me. This is the lesson that I learned through this. It is said, "You can't worry and trust at the same time." And I'm beginning to understand what Dr. Sara was trying to get across to me.

I have to go in for a chemo treatment, so my mom drops me off. Later, Dr. Sara has my mom come in to talk about how I am doing, and what has to be done to make sure that the cancer will not spread. Dr. Sara takes her into the big room, and they bring me in. She is sitting on a stool waiting for me. When I follow Danny into the room for my treatment, I'm surprised to see her there. I smile as she says, "There's my boy."

She sees how good I am being with Danny. He gets down on the floor with me, and with help from another nurse, puts the catheter in, starting my treatment. I feel like such a big boy, behaving so good and my mom sees all of this. As she watches, I can tell she is very proud of the way I'm handling myself, because she can't stop smiling at me.

Later that day my mom's at the computer sending an email to Dr. Sara,

Subject: Quinn...... "*Sara, I noticed that Quinn is favoring his foot. Holding it up in the air. Not wanting to put pressure on it. What's up with that?*"

Sara emails back. "*I'm not sure---let's give it a day or so---does he still have antibiotics?*" S Subject: Re: Quinn.... "*Is that the Ciprofloxacin? He has 24 of them.*"

She again answers the email, "*Yes it is and good, I'm glad you have it. Was he romping or anything last night?*".My mom emails back. "*I did see him take off in a full blown run from the yard to the gate. But he seems to be okay yesterday and this morning. We are outta power mushrooms; does he need more of those? Does he need the acid reflex still? He didn't pee last nite, but yesterday was his "off-day" for the pred. This morning he gets one, so I know how the pattern is going. Pill in the morning, that night he pees.* Dr. Sara emails back, "*Yes to the mushrooms. No to the acid reflux stuff. Happy that he is happy.*"

My medication must be working, as I have been feeling really good lately. My tail is constantly wagging at my pals and my mom. And I can't stop from grinning all the time. Life is good, and I'm a happy boy. I love my mom and my family, and all my dog friends at obedient school, my best friend, Dr. Sara, along with all my friends at the clinic. My days here can't be any better than this.

Now that the days are hot and the nights are warm, we still get to sleep in at night. Except that at night, the front door is always open, with a swamp cooler keeping the house comfortable for us. This way we can come in and out whenever we feel like it. Our buckets are full of cool water.

Every other day my mom has me lay down on the carpet, where she puts a big towel down to change my wrap. She unwraps the bandages, looking at the wound where the tumor and toe were. She then puts some Silvadene cream on it, and that makes it feel good to me. She wraps it with gauze and finishes it off with either a blue or red colored elastic wrap. Sometimes I get a wrap from the vets that has pictures of doggie bones on it. When my auntie Terry wraps my foot, it *stays* wrapped. Sometimes after my mom wraps it and I'm running hard with my pals, it will come off. My mom was cleaning my foot today, when I got a peek at how it looked. My other middle toe has moved to the center of my foot. It looks funny without any fur on it. They had to shave that spot for the surgery. So when the wrap is off, it looks like I have three paws and one emu claw. And this makes my mom laugh. I love it when she laughs, cause then it makes me wag my tail.

My appointments to see Dr. Sara have slowed down from two a week to just one, and it is now going into July.

My mom emails to Dr. Sara on July 1, 2008 Subject: Quinn…
..*"Yesterday a friend of mine came by after not seeing Quinn for a couple of weeks, and said that he looked so different. Looked happy and acted like he was a new boy. But we KNOW that anyway. So now on his "off" day, when he doesn't take the pred, he is only taking the Salmon oil (still outta mushrooms) is this right? See ya tomorrow."* Dr. Sara emails back.
"I think the power mushrooms are back--yeah--we knew he was a happy boy,",..S,

Tues. July 15, 2008, my mom emails Dr. Sara: Subject: Quinn…
"Sara do you want me to unwrap his wrap first thing in the morning or just before we come in for our app?" "Just before you come in. S

My mom tells us dogs that this week-end we will be going camping. I've never been camping before, so I don't have a clue what that means. But Ernie knows, and I've got to say, that guy is going nuts, thinking about what is going to happen. He tries to run it down to me, what we'll be doing. He doesn't know exactly where we are going, but says we get to sleep out in a forest somewhere.

Before Rosey came to live here, he said that Mae and that other Rottweiler, Morton II, and he went camping up in Tahoe National Park.

"Boy, did we have a time!" he said with delight.

He went on to tell me that the campsite was not like other campgrounds, where there are people all over the place, but that they were out where there are wild animals. My mom and her friends had to build a fire pit and find a place away from the main area to use as a potty spot. In a camp-ground with people, we have to be on a line or leash at all times. But out in the forest we could be off leash, as long as we stayed in and around our campsite. I can't wait til tomorrow gets here, and we can leave for our camping trip.

The next morning, my mom is busy packing the car with all of the stuff for our trip. There is so much camping gear that Rosey will have to ride in the other car that will be going with us. We are now heading out of town and turn onto a long and curving road that takes us west toward the coast. It doesn't seem like it's been very long before we pull up to the entrance to the campgrounds.

Now we're driving around, looking for the other friends that'll be camping with us. They had gone ahead and picked out our spot. First thing my mom does is let us out to take care of business. Then she has to fix a long line between a big tree and the table leg, where she will tie our leashes. The water buckets are setup for us and she gets our food bowls ready for when we come back from going down to the river. We are running along smelling all of the different smells from animals and things that people have left behind. She doesn't want me to get in the water, because of my wrap. Even though she has more wrap with her, it's best that I keep it dry. But dogs being dogs, the next thing I know, I'm running in the water following my pals along the edge. After my mom and her friends look for different kinds of rocks, we head back to camp.

My mom gets our food ready and we eat. When we are finished, she takes us one by one for a potty walk. I get to go with my mom all around the camp area, where I see kids riding their bikes with their dads. We come back to camp and my mom hooks me up next to Ernie and Rosey, while she and her friends have their dinner. It's dark now, and we have a big fire burning in the pit. While the others are laughing and joking around, we each get a separate walk around the campground before turning in for the night. On my turn, my mom and I could hear Rosey and Ernie barking at people going by close to our camp. They weren't behaving like good dogs should, so we had to cut our walk short and go back. It's time to go to bed and those two will not stop making a racket. Because of this we have to come into the tent with my mom and sleep there. It's a good thing she has her own tent. Otherwise it wouldn't be possible for all of us to be in there together. I do not understand the way these guys act. When someone walks by our gate at home, they start barking. So they think that they can do this when we're camping. That really gets my mom. She is always telling them to: "Leave it!!" I act the same way camping as I do at home. I just stand there looking at the people walking by, wagging my tail in a lighthearted way at them, and no way barking.

I want to set as good an example as I can, about how a Rottweiler should act. It seems like there are more bad ones out there than good ones. It's not our fault that we have this bad rap. It's because there are people who don't know how to handle us. Not everybody is the right person for my breed. If you are strict, but fair with us and don't give mixed signals, you will have a wonderful pet. Some Rottweilers are very hard, and because they didn't have proper training as young dogs, or when they were puppies won't be very good pets. Then there are ones like me, that are loves and all we want is to be the very best companions ever. In the beginning when I went to my new veterinarian, I wasn't the best Rottweiler. That was because I hadn't been given the right training about how to behave at a animal hospital. After my mom and Dr. Sara, along with the talks from my pet family, I turned out to be a good boy. I was lucky, as some would have given up on me. And then I would have forever had a bad name. Nobody at a pet clinic wants to have to muzzle a dog every time he comes in for a treatment or a shot. And I know my mom would never have let me continue the bad behavior.

The next day we spend playing along the river bed, chasing sticks and just being dogs. Soon it was time for us to head back home. If Ernie and Rosey had not been barking at everybody, we could've stayed another night. My mom says that I'll be able to go camping again without those two. But she doesn't really know what she would do with them. How would she be able to leave them behind and just take me?

On one of those nights when she was telling me a story about her dogs, she told of when her and her daughter, and grandkids went camping on the coast at Wages Creek. She was watching a lady's Rottweiler, while they went away for the week-end. All together with her daughters dogs, and hers there were eight dogs. Everyone was tethered in and among the bushes and trees of our campsite. On Monday when the lady came to get her dog, she asked my mom if she did anything over the week-end, because it was Labor Day. My mom told her that she went camping with her family. The lady asked what did she do with her dog? My mom said that she took her along with all the other dogs. The lady's face turned kind of reddish. My mom figured that the lady and her family had gone camping, and since her husband didn't care for the dog, didn't want her along. So there would be no-way that Ernie and Rosey wouldn't get another chance to go camping.

Ernie is the one with his Terrier attitude that is the whole reason. When Mae would be on a walk with my mom and saw other dogs coming towards them, she never did anything wrong, like start barking or jumping at them. But when she was walking with Ernie and he started barking or jumping at other dogs, Mae would mimick him. Which made her look just as bad, even though she was a wonderfully obedient dog. Rosey can be good sometimes on her own, as she is still learning.

It's after lunchtime and my mom wants to start packing up the car and head back home. She's getting everything in the car, when she realizes that she's going to have to leave the ice chest so there will be room for Rosey. She takes it out and we all pile in. I'm the biggest, so Ernie and I get in the back and settle down, while Rosey jumps into the front seat next to my mom. Off we go out the entrance of the campgrounds onto the highway, heading south-east towards Booneville, and then we turn onto Rt. 253 to Ukiah. Even though the trip will take us less than an hour, it's the best car ride I ever had. When we drove over the other day, I thought I was in Heaven. I don't remember ever getting to go for a ride that lasted that long.

We now are back home and in the gate. We get out and run around the yard, while my mom unloads the car. After our dinner we lie down to take a snooze. All I can dream about is the wonderful time I had, running along the river, playing with my pals and going on walks with my mom. Oh, what a lucky guy I am.

It's been a week since my mom took my buddies and me camping. Today it is starting out hot again, so we don't get to play with our toys, running after them as much. I have a hard time cooling down. Because Rottweilers have black coats, hot weather is not the best. Rosey seems to handle the hot days okay, and she's as black as I am. My mom will turn the hose on to sprinkle the flowerbeds, and Rosey will run after the stream of water. As long as the hose is squirting back and forth she'll continue to chase it. My mom will squirt her in the mouth, and Rosey just loves it. The more she gets wet the better she likes it. Now, Ernie on the other hand see the hose being turned on and automatically thinks it's bath time. He's out of there and up on the porch in a flash.

We are lying on the lawn in the shade trying to keep cool, when I see my mom dragging a big round blue thing across the yard towards where we are. As she gets closer, I notice that it's a kids wading pool. Ernie sees it at the same time I do, and says.

" Hey, I remember that pool from last summer, our mom would run water down that molded slide in it, and then it would get full. I don't like going in it, but Rosey loves the water."

Rosey hears what Ernie's saying and turns to see what he's talking about.

"Oh wow, I love laying in that tub. You can cool off really fast." I watch as my mom sets it on the lawn and makes sure it's level.

"Before I fill this pool, I want to take the wrap off your foot, Quinn." She says.

"I'm not sure if you're going to like going in there or not, but I don't want you getting it wet."

She kneels down next to me, and start unwrapping it. The hose is lying in the bottom of the tub, and I can see the water slowly rising towards the top. She turns the water faucet off and reaches down in the water for the hose. As she pulls the hose out, she wiggles her hand in the water to make it ripple.

"Come on you guys, don't ya want to play?" She laughs as she's scooping up some water and flinging it at us.

I stand there wagging my tail, as I watch her get Rosey wet a little. I'm pretty hot because the temperature is 102 degrees. So I limp over to the edge and stick my head down low enough to take a drink. Oh that water's so cold, it tastes wonderful. I really don't want to go in there, so I trot over to the kennel and lie down on the cool cement floor. This is the way to spend a hot day, just laying around with my pals in the yard. Ernie keeps whining something about dinnertime. He is sure that my mom has forgotten, because of the wading pool.

Annie is my friend staying with us.

CHAPTER 14

A BIOPSY

I couldn't eat anything last night, because this morning I have an appointment to see Dr. Sara. She wants to take a biopsy from the lymph node, and send it off to the pathologist who will examine it to see if there is any cancer. While I'm under the anesthetic, Dr. Sara is going to check my toe to see if it's clean of the cancer cells that were there before.

My mom is very worried about all of this. I see her go through all of her emotions; one minute she's sad, the next angry, or really mad. Because she pretty much knows what the outcome will be. She has gone through this with four of her other Rottweilers, and is hoping so much, that this time will be different. She says, it's so unfair that this is happening to me, and wishes somehow we could go back to the month of April, when I wasn't sick. Back to the dreams of all the things we were going to experience together. She was as happy as I was, at the way I fit right in with the other dogs and Lillie. She knew that there wouldn't be any problems, and that we would all get along. And on top of that, nobody had any serious health issues. Everything was okay with all of us. Ernie and Rosey never had any doggie sickness, and the same for Lillie.

The day has been a long one, not only for me, but also for Dr. Sara. And my mom is patiently waiting at home for the phone call telling her that I'm ready to come home. I hear someone coming to get me. I can hardly walk, because of the anesthetic. And it isn't wearing off very fast. My mom helps me to the car, where I fall into the front seat. She tries coaxing me into the back, but I can't pull myself up. She gives up and goes around to the drivers side, gets in. When we get home, she tries to get me out of the car and I can't move. I feel so awful, like I'm really drugged and moving isn't an opinion. She leaves the car door open, and goes into the house, hoping that maybe I'll get out by myself.

Later in the evening, she gets on the computer to email Dr. Sara.

. Subject: About Quinn

Boy was Quinn messed up. I tried to offer him some water to drink. And wipe his eyes. Every time I wiped his eyes, they would just water more. And his bottom-lids drooped like a Bloodhound's. In the morning I had to put a leash on to get him up to go outside. He was still out of it. I think he was sedated a little too much, cause he has not acted this way before. Talk to ya soon

Dr. Sara answers: Re: About Quinn

How is he doing today? He was under anesthetic quite a while (not as long as his original surgery, but still for a while) and lots of time we keep them in the clinic to sleep it off, but I always like to get them home, understanding that it hard for "moms" to see the recovery. He had less sedation than he had previously, but it so helps to get your feed back so I can note in his chart about delayed recovery. Today I hope we get our news. S

Later on Sara emails: Re:Re; Quinn

Toe does not have any cancer cells in it---waiting for lymph node--how is my boy?

My mom answers back: *You mean how is "Mr. Happy Boy"? I changed his wrap today, cause it was kind of coming off. Yesterday (Thursday) he seemed to be favoring it some. Using it lightly. So I'm not sure if it was his foot or the back of his leg that was bothering him. I gave him a dose of Metacam this morning, when he ate. And he is just the happy guy. So glad his toe is fine. Got my fingers crossed. Going with your gut feeling. And now his friend Sophie is here for the week-end. Chris told me about her leg. Gave me her meds and off he went. I feel like I got a dog clinic going on here. Can't wait to hear the results. Thanks for being my vet.*

The next day Dr. Sara gets the results of the tests. I have cancer cells in my lymph node behind my back left knee. She sends my mom an email about Quality Control:

I knew that what that meant was that they were just looking for quality of the staining process etc, but had already read the slides so I called my "inside" person this am and she went and looked and said...you will get this report tomorrow, they DID find mast cells in the lymph node. I burst into tears and said "are you sure, are you sure" and she said yes....

Sooo-cancer so sucks and can do whatever it wants, whenever it wants. Why does it target sweet souls like my parents and you and Teddy Kennedy and Quinn and Maple Rose when there are a zillion creeps in the world??? I know there isn't an answer to that one...I am so shook up and saddened and I know you are, but that's not gonna help Quinn and he wouldn't even understand why we were on such a bummer. So now what do we do? I have been online for 5.2 hours and this is what I know.

We would need to "stage" him again which means he NEEDS the abdominal ultrasound to see what his liver and spleen and lymph nodes look like. If they all look normal then we should take out the affected lymph node. If they are positive then there is no point in doing that. Time is always of the essence and so assuming we are going to head this way, he needs his ultrasound tomorrow or Tuesday, since my next procedure day is Wednesday and the lymph node could come out on that day if he is clean. He WAS clean before and hopefully that is still true, but these f'ing tumors can and do act unpredictably. Damn, I just wanted to assure this sweet, sweet big grumbly dog that life was worth living and that he would get plenty of it and that we were SOOO close....Damn, shit, and hell. S The Elsie Brown fund is donating $200.00 to Quinn..

I feel okay today, and I believe that my pain medication is doing it's job. I'm ready to play with my pals. My mom can tell that I'm feeling better, and so she gathers up our toys, to take us outside for some playtime. I take turns with Rosey like the other times that we play this game. Ernie is running around Rosey and me. He's smiling as he holds his yellow rubber bone in his mouth, and bouncing all around the lawn. I love this game so much. I drop that ball in front of my mom and she tries to fool me into which way she is going to kick it. I throw my front shoulders back and forth, rocking from side to side, trying to block the ball from zooming past me over the grass to the other side by the fence. Sometimes I have to take my foot and try to scratch the ball out of the berry-bushes, so I can pick it up in my mouth and carry it back to my mom. This is where we start all over again with her trying to bluff me. All I can do is smile, because I am having so much fun. Then I go for one more run out to get the ball and slip on the grass. Wow I'm thinking as I stand back up, I feel like I did something to my left front leg. This is the one with the arthritis in it. But I have a lot of catching up to do, as far as my playing goes. So I will just push the pain in this leg to the back of my mind and have some fun.

I am eating a little bit more now, because my mom has been putting so many goodies in my food. She feeds me cooked carrots and cuts them up in tiny pieces. Sometimes I get broccoli and asparagus, and of course cottage cheese, along with regular cheese. And I can't forget the scrambled eggs, as they are a big favorite with me. Oh how I love this food.

Today I have to be dropped off at the clinic for my ultrasound. Dr. Sommers will be doing it. I'm barely settled in the kennel when Denise comes to take me into the big room. Up onto the table I go, being the best boy I can be for Dr. Sommers. I can tell that she's a gentle soul, by the way she looks at me, with a soft smile on her face. I'm under the sedation now, and an x-ray is being taken. She's going to do a ultrasound to see if any of the cancer has gotten into my organs or not, and check my other lymph nodes, because the lymph node behind my knee has cancer cells.

Afterwards my mom comes to get me, as she sees that I'm again a mess. This is beginning to wear on my mom somewhat. When she gets me in the car, she turns around to unclip my leash. Saying to me,

"Quinn, this is the last time we're doing this. We're going home and have a great dinner with chunks of chicken in it. I just can't put you through this anymore."

After dinner my mom goes online to check her email. There's a message from Dr. Sara:

RE: Quinn *His sub-lumbar node is enlarged and likely has mast cell in it--he needs chemo today. Can you come in at noon? Me*

Sitting and staring at the computer for what seems to be forever, my mom looks at me with a tired expression on her face. She slumps in the chair, putting her hands up to her face and covering her eyes. Several minutes go by before she takes her hands away and says to me, "Sara wants you to come in for a chemo treatment, and maybe it will help you, so lets go."

Well I'm all for a ride in the car, and a visit with my friends at the clinic, so off we go. Today will be the start of chemo cycle #1. First I get a treatment this week, and then next week my mom will give me four chemo pills to take. She is so good at giving pills, and that Rottweilers are the easiest out of all her dogs. She says our mouths are like huge canyons, that she can stick her whole hand down in there, pushing the pills to the back of the throat with one hand and rubbing it down on the outside with the other. The following week, Dr. Sara will do a CBC- complete blood count, which will evaluate my red and white blood cells, to determine if there's any thing wrong.

Ernie laying on the lawn.

CHAPTER 15

MAST CELL TUMOR

I got my treatment, and my mom came to take me home. It will be three weeks before I go back for Dr. Sara to do my blood work. I spend the days doing all the doggie things that I so love, playing with the other dogs, teasing Dakota through the gaps in the fence; (while all the while, really wanting to be friends with him,) running up to the gate just to watch the people walking by with their dogs, never to harass and bark at them like Ernie and Rosey do. And going for walks down to the park with my mom. The dog classes have stopped for now. These August days have been very hot, so my mom keeps us comfortable by only playing early in the mornings and later in the evenings, when it cools down.

The only time I don't feel like eating is after a chemo treatment, and when I take my four chemo pills. The chemo probably causes the same reaction in dogs as it does in humans. My mom said it was awful when she had her treatments. She would come home and just sit straight on the edge of the couch, not moving a muscle one way or another. Some times when her dinner was in front of her, she would take one look at it and jump up and run to the bathroom. It made her mad, she told me. Because my mom loves dinnertime, the same way Ernie does. I'm laughing at the thought of him as it gets closer to two o'clock.

That pain medication, called Metacam seems to work the best. My mom measures out the amount that's right for me, and then squirts it into my food. With the cottage cheese in there I can hardly taste it. But she still has to coax me into eating all my food. At dinnertime I just don't want to eat. This makes her worry about what's going on.

This chemo is taking a toll on my system. My days are sometimes up or down, depending on what time of the day or night I take my medication. When I first take it, it helps the pain go away. But the problem is still there. And when I run and play I don't notice it until a little bit later. That's when I have to limp, because it hurts so bad I can't put all of my weight on that leg, and it's not time for my next dosage. There are few days where I don't have to limp to get around. The days that my leg hurts, I go down to bed. Or I shove the pain to the bad of my mind, so I can play.

At night I sit in front of my mom, offering her my paw like always. I love doing this, because when I do she'll tell me stories about her other dogs. Tonight she's telling us that Annie is coming again to spend the week-end. Her family is going to Sacramento, to look for a new house. I'm excited, 'cause I love Annie. I like it when she tells me about her life before she came to live with her wonderful new family.

It isn't long before Annie arrives at our house. I stand back as Ernie and Rosey are jumping and sniffing all around her saying their hellos. Being a little shy, I don't want to be pushy like the other two. I wait my turn, until she notices me standing over to the side of the driveway. She gives me a big doggie grin, as I do the same.

"Good to see you Annie, I've missed you." I say to her.

"Same here, Quinn. You look good."

"I'm okay, except my leg has been bothering me a lot lately."

"What's wrong with it" she asks as she stares at my leg and foot. "What is that bootie thing on your foot?"

"I had a Mast Cell tumor, and my doctor had to remove it and one of my toes. And my mom likes to keep it wrapped sometimes."

"Oh how awful, are you okay now?"

"I've been going for chemo treatments, and taking some pills, because the Mast Cell tumor is in one of my lymph nodes, behind my knee on the same leg as my bad foot." I'm explaining.

"Dr. Sara emailed my mom about my sub-lumbar node being larger than it should be, and I probably have Mast Cells there. So Dr. Sara and my mom are upset about this and are trying everything they can."

I'm so sorry Quinn, I hope everything will be okay, and you'll be well again."

She comes over to me and rubs her nose on my cheek, as my mom is calling us to come in the house. Annie is a sweet girl and a trusting friend. I'm glad I know her.

The week-end seemed to have flown by so fast, and now it's Monday. Annie's mom will be coming to get her later this afternoon. Rosey has been sneezing since yesterday. I feel sorry for her. First she sneezes and then rubs her nose on the carpet.

I ask her, "Hey, Rosey are you alright?"

"I don't know....it feels like I got something up there, and it's bugging me."

The sneezing goes on all evening. Just when my mom thinks that Rosey's okay, she starts sneezing again.

Now that it is nine o'clock in the morning, my mom is on the phone to the vets. She only has to push "dial 3" and it rings. They answer and put my mom on hold. My mom is waiting for a nurse to pick up the call, when she hears, "are you being helped?"

My mom recognizes Sara's voice on the other end, and explains what is happening with Rosey.

"Bring her in now and we'll look at it,… good-by." My mom thanks Dr. Sara. Rosey will have to be left there for the day, as she doesn't have an appointment. So Ernie and I spend the day waiting for Rosey to come back, sniffing around the fence between our yard and Dakota's. There are critters that live in the roots of the ivy. Every once in a while Ernie will find a hole that is used for the entrance to their home. Back and forth we go, sniffing and looking up into the dense leaves. I can really smell their scent, but can't quite figure out where they're hiding. I go back and forth along the fence, trying to see if I can get a glimpse of whatever this critter is.

Sometimes I hear the dead vines from the ivy breaking, making a snapping noise. Then I hurry to where the sound came from hoping to catch this varmint. I wonder what my mom would think of me if I presented her with my catch? Ernie now is a different kind of hunter. He goes to the hole and starts digging and sticking his nose and head in it all the way up to his ears. When he comes up for air, his face is covered in dirt. He's a funny guy, when he catches a scent, he will start making this yappy high pitched barking, whiny sound. The same one he uses when he hears the fire trucks. Ernie being a hound-mix, will make this sound when he is on the hunt. Hunting is a natural instinct for dogs, some more so than others.

My breed are not hunters, but workers. My ancestors drove cattle to the butcher's shop. The butcher would put his money in a pouch hanging around the dogs neck. Then the dog would race back over miles and miles of countryside, without anybody trying to take the money. They also were used to pull draft-carts for their owners. If Rottweilers work today, it's in search and rescue, or as police dogs. We're not as fast as German Shepherds, because we are a heavier dog, but we can bring a bad guy down in a blink of an eye, and he can't get loose from the grip we have on his arm or leg. It's not until the handler calls us off that we'll let go. I would never have made it as a police dog, as I love everybody. And I don't think I could really bite anyone. I showed them that at the clinic. I did give off good warning sounds though. The only reason for that was because I was scared, and didn't realize the doctors and nurses at the clinic were trying to see what was wrong with me. After it sunk in what they were doing, I was always a good boy for them. Being good was and is the thing I want to do at all times.

Ernie and I are called to the kennel, so my mom can go get Rosey. The clinic has called, and she's ready to come home. They said that she didn't have anything in her nose, but something had been in there. Her nose had to be flushed out, because it had gotten infected. During the evening Rosey whined a couple of times. I noticed that she would just stand there in the middle of the living room looking like she didn't know where she was.

"Rosey are you okay?" I asked her.

"I don't know, I feel strange and my head and nose feel funny." She whined back at me.

"I hope it wasn't one of those foxtails that fly through the air."

I'm telling her. "They can be horrible to a dog."

They have those little pointy parts, that make them only go one way, forward and they can't be pulled back out, if you try to pull on them, they might break off and the pointy end keeps on going.

It's the last day of August and the temperature has dropped down from 100 degrees to the low 90's. It's early so we can play ball for a short time. Ernie and Rosey are doing their same old game of catch with my mom. And I'm having a great time trying to trick her into throwing the ball one way or the other. I'm such a happy boy when I play ball with my mom. I do wish our yard was wider, so I could run farther. There's nothing like running. I know if we played in the back yard there would be more room to run. But I think my mom plays with us in the front yard, that way I don't run as far, because of my leg. I don't care which yard we play in, just so I get to play with her. It makes me happy when I see her smiling at me, and I always give her a wag of my tail and grin back at her when I drop the ball in front of her. I'm always thinking oh please don't stop because you see me limping. My shoulder and front leg would always be hurting me even if I didn't have the cancer in my lymph node in my back leg. I've got to remember that I can't get as excited as I do when I'm playing, because I always end up sliding on the grass. When that happens, I usually end up landing on my bad shoulder, like I just did now. Oh, ouch that one hurt pretty bad. My mom sees what just happened and stopped the playtime.

"Quinn, oh man are you okay?" She says to me.

I want to cry, as I hold my front paw up in the air. I try to put my weight on it, and a sharp pain shoots up my leg. Oh how I wish this wasn't happening to me. All I want to do is run and have some fun with my mom and my buddies, but in stead I hobble up the stairs into the house and go down to bed. I'm done for the day.

My mom emails Dr. Sara about my blood work, because she hasn't heard from her. Dr. Sara apologizes. Because it was so normal, she spaced it, and didn't think about it anymore. But she still wanted to know if I was limping? Because I am, she wants me to come in on Friday. Not only to check my leg, but it is time for me to start my chemo cycle, # 2. Because I'm a good boy now, I don't need to be sedated anymore. I just go in there, grinning at them and being the happy guy I am. They can give me my treatment right there on the floor of the big room. Making everyone love me for being me.

My mom emails Dr. Sara. Subject: Quinn

"He's *really been favoring his left front leg. But it's like when he's got "time" to think about it. If he is running around, it seems fine. But on the other hand, he doesn't want to put any weight on it. Speaking of weight...94.2 lbs today. Do I come in next Friday for the pills?*

Dr. Sara answers back. Re: Quinn

Four cycles and then we look at the sub-lumbar lymph node again and if that is normal size we quit!!!!! And yes this is cycle #2. He was tender across the top of his toes on that foot---I didn't fiddle with his feet a lot because I don't want to ruin his and my relationship....take a good look all over that foot and just make sure something isn't in there...keep in the Metacam and a little rest (no running for a week) and massage. Doable? S

The next day my mom has to email to Dr. Sara about what is happening to me as I lay beside her on the carpet. She emails, Subject: It's 9:55 Sunday Morning

And Quinn is laying on the living room floor, only thing movin' is his wrapped foot. He keeps moving it back and forth, like it is really bothering him. It's been an hour and he can't settle this leg-foot. When he gets up to walk, he puts very little weight on it. Then he lays back down and is moving his foot trying to get it comfortable. I'm sitting here watching him move his leg....back and forth......over and over. Doesn't seem like the Metacam is doing anything, as it's been over 2 ½ hours since he took it. It's now 1 pm and when standing, he is not putting any weight on it. It wasn't until he ate dinner @ 2pm that he finally stopped adjusting his leg (foot).

From: Sara Rice comes a reply, Re: It's 9:55 Sunday *Morning Well it must be more than that area you found on his foot--sounds like he needs an x-ray...I am working Tues. through Friday this week. Go in tomorrow if it seems severe, otherwise make arrangements to drop him off on Tuesday (I am in surgery the whole day, so they won't be able to make an actual appt.---let them know I WANT to see him. S*

It's the start of a new week and I'm feeling okay, I can ignore the pain in my back leg from the cancer "working" on my lymph node. I have had a great day today. Because of this my mom knows that Dr. Sara will want an up-date of what is going on, this is so she can make a note of my progress, and how I'm doing.

My mom sends an email, Subject: Quinn "It *must have been from when he was running around. Because like I said yesterday that after he ate, he finally stopped adjusting his leg. And today he is walking fine. I'll still be watching him more than not. So I feel ok with him not going in to see you. If anything isn't right I'll be in touch.....for sure. Mt* Dr. Sara emails back. Re: Quinn 10-4..S

My mom calls the clinic today to get me in to see Dr. Sara. When she comes back to get me, Dr. Sara tells her that the bump that is growing on the back of my leg is the "bad guy". So they will continue to give me the pain medication, the chemo treatments, the pills. I've also been taking some herbs, and some Power Mushrooms all along with the rest of my treatments. My mom knows that as long as I'm wagging my tail and smiling at her, and running to the gate with my canine family, that I am okay. She is praying every day that I will get well, and all the things that they have been doing for me will kill the cancer. That I will have a couple of more years to be here with her.

The next day is the day I get my four chemo pills. The chemo is doing some things to me besides killing the cancer cells. Some of my coat is falling out, all over the house. My mom is vacuuming a lot more than she usually does. She will sit out on the bench part of the porch and run the comb through my coat. As she combs me over and over, she puts the dead hair in a paper bag she has set beside her. Denise told my mom that my hair might come out a bit, because some of the chemo went into the tissue. And the white on my black coat is there again. My mom wraps my foot because she knows that it is bugging me. She like to leave it on for two to three days at a time. Then she takes it off, until it looks like it is bugging me again. I have been outside with Ernie and Rosey playing. We will be in the front yard, romping around with each other playing our doggie tag games that I love to do so much with them. Or race over to the gap in the fence to harass Dakota. Those two do the harassing while I stand back and watch. When they are through, I go to peek in the hole through the ivy. That's when out of nowhere Dakota lunges the fence, banging into it, like a Mack truck plowing into a tree. making it jolt a little. That scares me so much that I jump back away from the shaking fence, with my heart pounding very hard, deep in my chest. At the same time I'm worrying about what will happen if someday that fence comes crashing down.

I guess with all the running around, and those darn chemo pills I had to take, I don't feel so good this morning. My mom fixes me a really good breakfast with cottage cheese, but I don't want it. She is very upset about this, and takes my bowl away. She is cutting up some vienna sausages, it looks like she is going to put the whole can in this time, as she adds them to the mix. Putting my bowl back down on the plastic "stand" in the kitchen, she coaxes me to please eat this. I don't feel like eating at all, but because she is insisting so much, I want to make her happy. So I eat half of it, and this makes it okay.

My mom takes me to see Dr. Sara, because nothing is really making me feel any better. Dr. Sara changes my pain medication again, but I just keep on limping. It's getting harder and harder to hide this from my mom. She knows more about what is happening with me than I do. Hope and prayer are the things she is hanging on too. One thing that is a dead give away is when I'm laying on the living room floor by myself, and Ernie and Rosey are laying up by my mom at the computer. I would be up there also if I felt better. Then I get up and go down to my nice fluffy blanket where I can be by myself. I don't want my mom to see that I am in so much pain. But I know she knows what is up when I do this. Sometimes she calls me to come back up. I will do it, if I'm not hurting too badly. That's when I try my hardest to hide the pain, and wag my tail at her. I then sit in front of her and give her a big grin and shake her hand. She will usually tell me to lay down, which I do, until I notice when she is back to being occupied by something. Then I quietly get up and head back downstairs. I don't feel like coming back upstairs until I hear her say that it's time to go outside. It is the last time we go out before we go to bed. And then we can have our last cookie treat for the night. Sometimes, lately, it feels like it is getting harder to even do this. I'm beginning to think that I just may not win this battle. When I'm laying on my blanket my memory travels back to when I was laying on the blanket with the holes in it. On the cold cement floor of the shed. Who knows where I'd be if my mom hadn't adopted me. I have had the best care I could have ever thought possible.

Because of my limping still, my mom emails Dr. Sara, Subject: Quinn

Sara, Quinn is limping, limping, limping. The pain pills don't seem to be doing very much. He does take off with the other two up the driveway, and then as he is trotting back down the driveway, he looks like he has one leg shorter than the others. He is still "smiling" and wagging his tail.. But does choose to go downstairs by himself. It seems like he doesn't want tp put any weight on his foot. Does it sound like he needs another x-ray? Sara answers the email, Re: Quinn

It sounds like he does need an x-ray.. Call when you can and I can always get him in..as you know.. he is my guy..S

My mom brings me into the clinic. Dr. Sara wants to give me a Adequan shot, to help my limping. It is used mainly for arthritis. It was first used on horses, with good results. I hope it will help me. At first I though it did help, but it has only been three days and I am back to my front leg and shoulder, and back leg killing me again. My mom is a basket-case, worrying over me. It hurts me to see her so sad that she can't make it better.

Dr. Sara sends an email to my mom. Subject: Quinn

I am so bummed (as I know you are) about Quinn's lameness.--I was hoping the Adequan would be helpful, but obviously it is not. I am suspicious the one of those little bone chips has moved into an area of the shoulder joint that causes pain when he bears weight--it seems that before they were there, but not on a weight bearing surface. I don't know what else we can do for him right now..I have sent x-rays to my favorite surgeon, but there isn't anything I can suggest in the mean time, except maybe add some more Tramadol..I should see him this Friday for his CBC.. S

CHAPTER 16

Chemo Is Half Over

The days aren't as hot as they were, because it is getting to the end of September. But it's a little to warm to play chase the ball, so my buddies and I are laying on the lawn. We are very bored, but it's better laying here catching up on a little daydreaming, to while the day away. I open my eyes to see my mom dragging out the lawn-mower. She is going to make us get up and go lay in the kennel, while she mows the lawn. I never had any lawn to lay on before, so I love doing that, although the kennel floor is very cool, because it is cement. And my mom cleaned the kennel just a little while ago, so when she hosed it off, it really made it cooler for us. When it is to hot for us to play, my mom will try to catch up on her flower-beds. She sure loves working in her garden. Sometimes when I'm not napping because of the heat. I will just lay in the shade of the catalpa tree and watch her. Just laying there smiling at her, while Ernie and Rosey are laying on their sides, fast asleep. They are so used to what my mom does, and has been doing for as long as they have been here, they don't even think twice about it. I love everything about my home, and family, and I want to do nothing but soak it all up.

I am laying on the living room carpet, while my mom is giving me a tummy rub. Scratching me behind my ears, and on my chest. This feels so good, I don't want her to stop. She slows down and rubs her hand over my tummy again, feeling a small bump. "Oh Quinn, I don't know if this is bad or what? But you have a bump here." As she touches it.

She goes to the computer and sends Dr. Sara a email. Subject: UH-OH *I was giving our guy a tummy rub….on his stomach is a round, soft bump. Size of one of those peppermint candies. Flat not like those "fatty" ball soft bumps, that dogs sometimes get. When cancer cells metastasize, do they spread out from the primary tumor, or can they "jump" out to another spot? Shouldn't the chemo be killing these "bad" cells? I feel bad….most of the time now he goes down-stairs by himself. He'll come up when it's cookie time. Will lay with the others and me. Then will get up & go back downstairs.*

Dr. Sara answers, Re: UH-OH!!!
It could be a metastasis or it could be something else…I'll have to look at it….we would hope the cancer cells get killed by our drugs, but there are cells that are not sensitive to any drugs and those cells succeed and can spread. Quinn's nausea may be due to his chemo--let me know how it goes today…S

This month I have five vet appointments, and at the same time I'm halfway through my chemo treatments. I hope when this is all over that I will be able to eat like I'm supposed to, and all the pain will also be gone. I hate going down to my bed, and not stay upstairs with my buddies and my mom. I was brought into this family to be a part of it, not be by myself, down where nobody knows where I'm at. But the way I feel most of the time now, it's best to be down on my blanket. On hot days that is the place to be, as it is cooler, and upstairs is hotter.

Today I started chemo cycle #3, and am home now after spending the day at the vets and Dr. Sara. I may or may not see Dr. Sara when I'm here all day for a treatment, because the nurses also can do that for me. This is just as fun, since I get to see my friends there. Every once in a while, someone will come by and give me a scratch on my head or behind my ear. They try to make me as comfortable as they can. I stay until they can call my mom to come and get me. This chemo is making me feel sick to my stomach. I decided I was going to lay on the carpet near my mom after I got home from the vets, wanting to see if I could hang out with my pals. Then for some reason, this weird feeling came over me, fast like a surging tidal wave and I stuck my neck out as far as I could, just in the nick of time. When out flew my breakfast all at once. Ohhhh....this is not good. It felt like someone took a big boot and slammed me right in the stomach, really hard. I am very sick now, and I have to go down to my bed. It's not normal for a dog to behave like this. Dogs don't want to be by themselves, they want to be with their people, wherever they are. Some dogs are like Ernie and even follow their person from room to room. I have seen him follow my mom into the kitchen and just stand there like he is a statue, not moving, kind of like in a trance of some sort. When my mom takes a step, he opens his eyes to see what she is going to do. He watches to see if by any chance a crumb from a human cookie might hit the floor. Or fried chicken flakes, bread crumbs; anything will do. He's like a vacuum with his nose to the floor, sniffing back and forth. No matter what room my mom is in, he's there as well. He'll be laying in the living room, with one eye aimed on her, and the other one closed. He is good when he's in the kennel and my mom has to leave; he alternates from sitting straight up, looking through the kennel gate, towards the carport; to curling up on the roof of the doghouse or on the rug on the kennel floor. No matter which, when he hears the car coming up Standley St. echoing through the trees along the creek, he immediately goes and sits, waiting for the car to pull into the carport. He knows it's our mom, but he looks nonstop towards the porch, staring and waiting for her to come into his view.

Rosey handles being in the house about the same as spending time in the kennel. If she's in the house, she finds a spot that feels comfortable to her. Sometimes she lays with her back braced against the couch or a chair, and her legs up in the air. She will stay in this position for however long she feels like, then she rolls over into the classic position of a dog laying on one hip, and her head resting on her front legs, with her eyes closed. She is right on the edge of sliding into a nice little nap. when here comes Lillie, after bouncing off the kitchen counter onto the floor. Hardly making any sound at all; in a very soft cat-like way, she tip-toes across Rosey's head. Rosey is so cool about this; she just raises one eyebrow, opening just enough to see the tip of Lillie's tail heading out the cat door. That Lillie is one fast cat. My mom says she is a very fast hunter. She onetime downed a bat, and another time caught a hummingbird.

CHAPTER 17

Vienna Sausages

Something has grabbed Ernie and Rosey's attention as they mingle around the coffee table, letting my mom know that maybe she should let them out. They caught a scent of something out there and have to go take care of business. As they race out the front door, Lillie comes flying in through her cat door, at about 90 miles per hour in cat speed. She is leaning way to the left, as she clears the small opening, rounding out the curve of her track past the couch, finishing this race up on the counter top at her food dish. I hear all of this going on as I lay down stairs on my blanket. I want to be upstairs with my family. They sound like they are having a great time. This is good and they enjoy the home they have. I hear my mom say that it's time to go out for the night, meaning after that happened we get our cookies!

She calls me. "Quinn, come on....Quinn lets go!!"

I pull myself up, and at the same time try not to put any pressure on my front leg. I'm not sure just which leg hurts me the nastiest. My front leg hurts when I put weight on it. And my back leg aches deep inside; a nagging pain, that sometimes gets eliminated when I take my medication. I heard Dr. Sara tell my mom, she can give me my meds every eight hours, if need be. I slowly limp up the stairs one step at a time. There is a landing with a wider step at the bottom. And then only six steps up to the top. Finally I reach the top step and then one more up into the living room, and I am here. Phew, that took a lot out of me. But I manage to wag my tail a couple of times at my mom, letting her think everything is fine. And because I'm wagging my tail, smiling at her, that is just what she thinks.

The front door is open and Ernie and Rosey are already outside, when I finally make it out onto the porch. I head over between the shop and the house to take care of business. I don't think I could get down the front steps to the lawn with both my front and back legs bothering me like they are. We come back in and get our cookies for the night. I get my pain pill, and thank goodness, my mom is giving it to me earlier. So this means that I'll get it every eight hours. Hope it makes me feel better, as I snuggle down into my blanket, smashing part of it into a bunched up lump for a pillow. I stretch out really long across the blanket on my good side, and drift off to dream about running down at the field. My mom hardly takes me for walks lately. The other day she started up the street with me, and noticed that I wasn't moving right and came back to our driveway and turned into it. I so wanted to go for a walk. She has been babying me more than not.

Dr. Sara told her to, "Just let him be a dog!"

Maybe if I don't limp, she will take me down to the park. The only trouble is that my lymph node is very swollen, along with my foot, and I can't fake that there's nothing wrong. It hurts me too much.

We had to be kenneled today, because Lillie had an appointment with Dr. Sara for her annual health visit. I heard my mom say that Lillie needed a feline rabies shot. Cats need rabies shots just like dogs. They might be out in the yard, and get into a fight with a wild critter. And if that critter had rabies, it might get transmitted to the cat.

It seemed like only a short time before we hear the car pull into the driveway. My mom drives down to the carport and gets out with Lillie in her cat-carrier. In the house, Lillie is let out. Then the gate is opened for us. Ernie and Rosey, always get a head start on me. They are up, onto the porch, while I'm still trotting across the lawn to the stairs. We all run inside to see if Lillie is in one piece. She is perched up on the window box, being very still. Ernie starts off asking her questions about what happened while she was gone.

"Hey, it seemed like you were gone longer than just a visit the vets, Lil."

Lillie blinks her eyes slowly....open....shut....open!!

"Our mom had to pay some bills, because it's the first of the month, or something like that."

She went on to tell us about her adventure, riding around in the car. Stopping at the doctor's office, and then the bank and because mom was out, she wanted to grab some stuff from the grocery store. She's somewhat organized, and doesn't like to make extra trips, if she doesn't have to. Lillie went on to say that at first, she was giving my mom an earful, by meowing at the top of her lungs. Even my mom tried to drown out her crying, by turning the radio up louder, but that didn't work. She said that my mom kept telling her that it would be okay. After leaving the vets and driving from one place to another, Lillie started to except the fact that no matter how much screaming she was doing it didn't make any difference. By the time the groceries were being put into the car, Lillie was beginning to turn into one of those cats that really do like being in the car. You can start a kitten off by giving it a ride, just like a puppy, and soon it will be fine in the car. But most people don't have the same feeling with their cat as they do with their dog, and don't think about taking their cat with them. So cats aren't as comfortable riding in a car as a dog. Lillie finished telling us all about her day and said she was very happy to be back home, then immediately took off to head outside. It will be another year before Lillie has to go back to the clinic. And most likely that same amount of time until her next car ride. Dr. Sara said that Lillie was in great shape.

My Mom read about some miracle treatment called Neoplascene. It's supposed to eat the cancer cells right off the leg. My mom emails Dr. Sara again, as she is very worried about me.

Subject: Quinn" *Sara, Quinn and I are coming in on Monday morning. He is REALLY favoring his foot. Fri I rewrapped it. The bump is bigger and nastier than before. I am sooo upset...just wish I could go back to the month of April, and nothing was or would be wrong. But damn,.... he's a Rottweiler, and this sucks. My heart is broken and am having a hard time not to cry".mt*

The reply from Dr. Sara was: Re: Quinn

"I spoke to the Neoplascene guy (quite a talker) and all the items are on their way to me. Should arrive quickly.. if you can, wait until this arrives

to come in. Give him the Tramadol--you can do 2 tablets every 8 hours if needed…I am hoping, hoping that this new medicine provides us with a miracle"…S

My mom talks to Dr. Sara about this stuff that came. Dr. Sara said that it looked like it would work on a tumor that was on the outside, not an internal tumor. It was pretty nasty, and my mom didn't like the way it had to be used. Dr. Sara wasn't as excited about it after she had a discussion with Dr. Sommers. Also, my mom would have had to watch it eat a hole in my leg, while she kept it clean. Whoa, I don't want my mom to have to go through that. Because this was a very aggressive cure, and a nasty one at that, neither of them wanted to put me through it.

My mom emails Dr. Sara, because we have an appointment on Wed to see her. Subject: Quinn *"Sara, hope your R&R was just what the doctor ordered. When is your surgery? And back to seeing patients? Things have been going along normally since we last saw you. At the same time there are subtle changes happening. I mentioned how Quinn will go downstairs to his bed, in the evening. And not hang with the "big dog"(me). Some nights he has been going down, coming back up, etc. Last week he went down during the day, and went to bed. Would come up when I called him, would go out to play w/ Ernie & Rosey. Today is #2 at Sandy & Ray's dog class, (we go to do something fun together) He was fine at class with the treats. Fri. he didn't care about his food in the morning, And this morning he turned away. Was able to make him eat some. But dinner was not happening. 8:00 potty break, he was down in bed. Every night is the same. The others jump up to go outside, and I have to call him, 2 and 3 times, before he comes up the stairs. Tonight he would not come up, so I could give him his Tramadol. So I broke up a couple of vienna sausages. ½ good one, ½ one with pill in it. Right away he could taste it, started spittin' out the sausage, yankin' his head back and forth. And man the saliva was flyin' everywhere. Foam, and more foam. I kept wiping his mouth. Got a water-squirt bottle and sprayed water into his mouth. More foam, the more water…more foam. I WAS SO WORRIED! After fifteen minutes or so, Quinn came upstairs, over to me and laid down beside me. When time was to go out for last call, he went along w/ the other two. Has been sleeping here all night. Don't think he is going to care about vienna sausages from now on."* M

Dr. Sara replied, Re: Quinn

"The R and R was truly restful and I did need it…the surgery is November 10 and I will be out for 6 weeks after that.…I can't even imagine it, but I can't imagine living with this chronic pain anymore either…we'll see you guys on Wednesday…I've missed Quinn!!" S

The first time I had pills in my vienna sausage was when my mom wanted to show a friend how to give me my medication. My mom's friend couldn't bring herself to stuff it right down my throat. So my mom took a vienna sausage, broke it in half with the pill in one half .The other half plain. It must have worked like it was supposed to, because I didn't taste anything, but the sausage. Because of my pain, and it was time for my medication, she came down to my bed and tried to give it to me there. She had a big mess to clean up after I spit it out. Like she told Dr. Sara, she didn't think I would be crazy about vienna sausages anymore, and she is right. I'm afraid that there will be a pill in one of them sometime. (I don't even want to risk it.) This friend of my mom told her that I just gobbled them down, with out any problem. Now my mom knows her dogs very well. If this was done to Ernie or Rosey, that is exactly how it would have happened. I do not eat anything fast like that. I want to taste what I'm eating. My mom knew in her heart that I probably didn't get my medication. She is a very smart woman--she was right; I didn't.

CHAPTER 18

FLOWERS FOR DR. SARA

I went in to have Dr. Sara check me over and look at the blood-work that was done. She was back from her R and R. What does this R and R mean, I wonder? This was the longest time that I didn't get to see Dr. Sara, and I think I was starting to miss her. She has become one of my favorite people. Outside of my family, she is my best friend. I hope she doesn't have to go on another R and R for a long time. Because if she did, I would probably have to go with her.

Dr. Sara wants me to come in today for my chemo treatment. I was just there, three days ago, but she needs to see me one more time before her surgery. This will be the start of my last cycle. Maybe when she comes back to work in six weeks, I will be cured, or she may have to start the cycles over again? I don't know about how many times the veterinarian has to do these treatments. This is the last of the four cycles. In the next week I will take my four chemo pills and then because Dr. Sara will be recovering from her surgery, I will see another veterinarian. I know the other ones; Dr. LaRue or Dr. Sommers will probably be one of the vets that my mom will bring me to see. She doesn't know the new one, Dr. Bennett, so she will stick with the ones she knows. Dr. Sara wants my mom to drop me off the first thing this morning, but my mom said that we have a dog class. So Dr. Sara told my mom to go ahead and bring me in after my class is over.

My mom and I hop into the car after she kennels Ernie and Rosey. Off we go to Sandy and Ray's dog class, getting there before anybody else has arrived. My mom is telling Sandy that I have a chemo treatment today. I have to be at the clinic after we finish here. Sandy asks my mom, "How are the chemo treatments working out?"

My mom says, "I just hope and pray that the cancer goes away."

She goes on to tell Sandy that my foot has no more cancer in it. But she keeps the wrap on because my foot is still sensitive. And she really doesn't like the way it looks. The fur isn't growing back and my nails look longer than the other ones, even though they are the same length. All I know is my leg hurts me most of the time; even the pain medication doesn't seem to do its job. Other times, I feel silly and goofy from the pills, don't feel like eating any breakfast or dinner. When my mom gives out the cookies, I will take mine into the living room and eat it really slow. The cookies taste so good; I find no trouble in eating them. Kind of like little kids telling their moms that they are too full to eat their vegetables, but seem to be able to find room for desert.

Dog class is one of the things that I really enjoy. I can go in and out of the weave poles almost by myself now, mostly because I'm a fast learner. And love going through the long tunnel. Every time I come out, my mom is standing there with a big grin on her face, laughing at how happy I looked. Wiggling my tail as fast as I can, I hurry back to the other end and do it all over again. Today my mom helped me walk across a board that was up off the floor a couple of inches. She had my leash in her hand, and was guiding me slowly one step at a time to the other side. It's a little tricky at first, but I did very well. Most of the other dogs are gone, and so my mom says good-by to Sandy and tells her that we will see her next week. We head to the clinic, where my mom will drop me off for my treatment. Later in the day she'll come back for me. She will be there waiting in the lobby for me as always.

I get excited as she says to me. "Want to go see Sara?

I smile and wag my tail at her, knowing there is a ride in the car for me, plus I get to see my favorite vet. We are off down the street, on our way to the clinic.

We enter the clinic and I get weighed. My top weight was 94lbs. My mom was really happy about that, but since my chemo treatments I have dropped some. Today I weigh close to 85 lbs, and that is okay because of what I'm going through.

My friends at the desk greet me with a big "Hi Quinn," and that makes me feel loved by all of them. I wiggle my tail and smile back at them. My mom sits down and talks back and forth with the girls, if they aren't answering the phone or waiting on another client. Pretty soon my auntie Terry comes and takes me in back, and I hear my mom say, "Be good Quinn, and I'll be back for you later."

Things have changed since I'm a good boy now. I love everybody in the big room. I can tell that they are friends of mine, because of how nice they are to me. They've always been nice to me, but because I didn't have good manners in the beginning, I made it hard on them and myself. I have to wait for my treatment, as there are other dogs and cats in the big room ahead of me. Some of them have had operations for one thing or another. There are three other dogs that Dr. Sara has been treating for cancer. One of them was a elegant looking Boxer, named Maple Rose. My mom said that she had seen Maple Rose one day in the lobby when she was waiting for Dr. Sara. Maple Rose's mom and Dr. Sara were talking. Maple Rose was going to be twelve years old soon, and Dr. Sara described her as "being such a lady." If a Boxer lives to that age, they are blessed. Big dogs sometimes don't live as long as little dogs. Like my buddy, Ernie will go on until he gets to be about fifteen years old or so. He thinks he may die from starvation, or the possibility of missing a meal will do him in.

My treatment is done now, and next week my mom will give me my four chemo pills. Then one of the other vets will do my blood work and see how things are going. We hope the cancer is killed so I can go back to being a happy playful guy, and won't be sick anymore. My life has pretty much been happy with my new family, going places, playing with Ernie and Rosey. And Lillie has let me be a friend of hers, also. I say *let* because cats rule the world in which they live. Lillie is even the boss of my mom. The only thing my mom gets after Lillie about is her wandering across the counter top, or when she won't use her scratching thing on the wall, to sharpen her claws. Instead, Lillie goes over to one edge of the couch, or the front of a chair and starts to dig her claws into the upholstery. My mom hears that and starts yelling, "No, no Lillie, use your scratch pad." Lillie will then dart off running through her cat door and out into the yard. Then she will sink her claws into the side of one of the trees.

Dr. Sara comes and gets me out of my kennel. She says to me, "Come on, Quinn, Lets go see your mom."

As she leads me out into the lobby, I see my mom laughing at the big grin on my and Dr. Sara's faces. We are quite the pair. Dr. Sara and my mom started talking about what was going on with me, as I lay there on the floor in front of them. As they talked, I kind of drifted off into a snooze, dreaming about what might be in my dinner tonight, and if I will be able to eat or not. It's not that I'm not hungry when it's time to eat, I just don't feel up to it because of the chemo. My snooze is interrupted by Dr. Sara and my mom standing up as they finish talking. I'm watching Dr. Sara tell my mom about what time her operation is on Monday. She says with a far away glimpse on her face, "It will be at 9:30, so think about me." Dr. Sara looks a little scared or unsure for a split second or two.

"You'll be just fine. I'll say a little prayer for you at that time." my mom says, as she notices the look on Dr. Sara's face at the same time I do. My mom then walks over to Dr. Sara and gives her a hug, telling her she will be okay and that she is a strong woman.

The week-end passed by with me not feeling so good. It's Monday morning, and time for breakfast. My medication has been cut down to almost nothing, so the little bit I have I still have to take; my mom opens my mouth and sticks a pill way down my throat. She then rubs my neck until the pills go down. She has put some cottage cheese in my food, hoping that I will eat all of it. As hard as I try, I just can't finish what's in my bowl.

My mom tells me that Dr. Sara's operation will be in a couple of hours and hopes everything goes well for her. She says to me, "Quinn since you care for your vet very much, how would you like to send her some flowers, to cheer her when she wakes up from the anesthetic?"

I'm remembering as I hear the word *anesthetic,* that's what I had during my surgery. I remember also the talks my mom and Dr. Sara had about how painful her knee had been for her. Pain is a very bad thing to live with. I have been in pain for most of the time that I've been fighting this horrible cancer. Not to mention the arthritis in my shoulder, which was there before the monster got a hold of me. Dr. Sara, my mom and I have been doing everything we can to stop it, so I can be well again. My mind comes back to the question my mom just asked me. Oh! I want Dr. Sara to wake up with something that will make her smile. I'm thinking a nice bouquet from her best boy will do the trick. I look at my mom and wiggle my stubby tail and grin at the same time.

"Okay, that must mean that you want to do this for her, right?" she asks me. "And how shall I have the lady from "Flowers by Annette" sign your card?"

Now, my mom and I have very good communication skills between the two of us. After looking at me carefully, trying to figure out what I'm thinking, she says "Okay. We will have her sign it, To: My favorite vet. From: Your favorite Rottweiler, Quinn."

I wiggle my stubby tail in agreement, as I like the thought of that. My mom's daughter lives and works in Willits where Dr. Sara's orthopedic surgeon practices, at the Frank R. Howard Memorial Hospital. The hospital founded by the automobile magnate, Charles Howard, who owned the Buick dealership in San Francisco. He also happened to be the owner of the great race horse of the 1940's, Seabiscuit. There is a huge ranch south of Willits called Ridgewood Ranch. That is where Seabiscuit lived after his racing career was over. Charles Howard had a son that was killed in an accident on the ranch. So Mr. Howard wanted to keep the memory of his son alive and in doing so give back to the community by building a hospital for the town of Willits.

This is a small town where everybody knows everybody. So when my mom's daughter, Bobbie, went to get my flowers for Dr. Sara. She told her friend Annette, who owns the flower shop what to put on the card. Annette laughed and asked "What's that all about?"

Bobbie told her about the fantastic bond that had formed between Dr. Sara and me, and how I was really good pals with her, and also about my chemo treatments and all. She told her I wanted to send Dr. Sara flowers to cheer her up.

"Oh how sweet that is, I never made a bouquet for any one that was sent by a dog before."

Bobbie went on to say that I wasn't just any dog, but one of her mom's Rottweilers. Anyone that knows about my mom and her Rotties, knows her Rotties are her world. And the reason that Ernie and Rosey live with my mom, not being Rottweilers, is because she knew that if she didn't take them in, something bad would probably happen to them. She has a soft heart, and wanted them to live where they wouldn't be tied to a tree. When the time comes for one of her Rottweilers to have to leave this earthly world, she respectfully waits for the right amount of time to pass.

Then a day comes along and she starts getting what she calls "Rottweiler with-drawls," and her search is on for one that is in need of a good home. It used to be that she had more than one living with her. At one time she had four Rotties living together. So there never was a time that she was without a Rottweiler. Mae was the last of the bunch. After Mae was gone, it was a whole year before she got Jazz. And then a year without a Rottweiler between me and Jazz. Before, me she found a female in the Lakeport SPCA, but didn't have a totally right feeling about her. She called Dr. Sara up and talked to her about this girl. Dr. Sara said that it might be a good match for my mom. And maybe this dog could be turned around? My mom came so close to adopting this dog.

This is one reason dogs end up at the pound or shelter, because the match isn't good. It's not fair to either the dog or the person. So people have to be sure that the family and everyone involved is right for each other. She then went looking on the internet, at Petfinders. She narrowed it down to an old guy over at the Sacramento SPCA. She drove over there to check him out, and again it wasn't a good gut feeling, so she drove home without a dog. The drive home was long and tiring for my mom. She was frustrated over the wasted day, as she stood in the kitchen scanning the pet column want-ads. Which is something she doesn't usually do. At the top of the page was my ad. It jumped out at her. BAM!! She stared at it for a moment, and then said out loud,

"Wow! You don't see ads like that very often, if ever. They're going to get a bunch of calls about him; I'd better call first thing in the morning."

That was how it all began. My mom believes that things happen for a reason. Whether or not for the good or bad of things. Maybe just to learn a lesson one way or another. So you see, had she taken either one of those dogs, I would have ended up with someone who might not have been a Rottweiler person, but just someone who wanted a Rottweiler. Most likely they would not have gone through all that my mom and Dr. Sara did to save me.

Dinnertime came and went for me. Ernie and Rosey wolfed theirs down without a problem. I tried my best to eat, even after my mom put in all kinds of yummy stuff. She looked so sad and was trying really hard to get me to eat, but I just couldn't do it.

When the time comes, we all get ready for bed. Ernie and Rosey settle down on their blankets and I push the top layer over until I can curl up with it bunched up against my back. I drift off to sleep, dreaming about my vet, wondering if she is okay, if she got the flowers sent her. I feel so proud that my mom asked me if I wanted to do that. Everybody knows that dogs need help with things like this, and I am happy that I could do that for her. She IS my favorite veterinarian in the whole world. I also know that she isn't really a Rottweiler person. She feels the same way about Boston Terriers that my mom does about Rottweilers. People in the dog world do that. They love dogs in general, but most of them have a favorite breed. Some may even love a couple of different breeds.

Morning is here and my mom gives out the cookies. Ernie and Rosey grab theirs in haste. I just sniff at mine and turn away. My mom lets the other two outside and fixes my breakfast.

I really feel sick today, more so than I have. My leg is killing me, and I'm waiting and hoping the pain pill will start to work. My mom sets my bowl down on the plastic tub for me to eat. I sniff at it, and oh, it smells so good. I can't even take a nibble or two. It is not going to happen. My mom is trying so hard to get me to eat and I won't, so she gives up. I turn and go downstairs to bed, it feels so nice. I love my bed, as I get flash-back of how it used to be in the shed. I hear my mom call me to come up stairs as she wants to play with us. I limp slowly up the stairs as I see my mom gather up our toys to take outside.

This was when I told my mom it was time for me to go

CHAPTER 19

Time Has Run Out

We go outside to play ball. Rosey is all over my mom to get her to throw her T-Rex for her, and Ernie is jumping all around, making Dakota angry and stirring him up, as always. He says, "Ha-ha Dakota we get to play and you don't," as he bounces all over the lawn carrying his toy in his mouth, chasing Rosey. My mom threw my ball over to the fence. I smiled as she did that for me, but I really don't feel like playing ball today, as much as I love doing this, because you have to remember this is my second favorite thing to do besides riding in the car. So I trot slowly after the ball and bring it back to my mom. Now Rosey is all geared up for play, as is Ernie. They are keeping my mom very busy, throwing toys for them. She gives my ball another kick to the other side of the yard, and now I just walk over to pick it up. Bringing it back is now very painful. My leg has shooting sharp pains. Okay, I'm thinking I don't know if I can continue this game anymore. One more time she gives my ball a kick, and I go after it. I pick it up and slowly carry it over to the porch and climb the stairs. I turn and with my ball still in my mouth, I watch Ernie and Rosey having so much fun. At this very minute, I have mixed emotions, both sad and happy. Sad because I am not up to playing my favorite game, and happy at watching my buddies having the best fun, knowing that there isn't anything right now that they would rather be doing.

About an hour goes by, when my mom hears the sound of a big truck backing in the driveway.

"The propane driver is here, come on and kennel." She yells at us.

Ernie and Rosey run to the kennel and jump up on the roof. I limp into the kennel, and turn around to see what is happening. I don't know what she is talking about.

Ernie shouts at me. "It's the propane man, bringing us gas for our stove."

"Huh, what do you mean?"

"At night when you get to sleep by the fire, well the propane is what burns in the stove."

He went on to say that the year he came to live here, our mom had a new propane stove installed. She used to have a wood stove, and after a couple of chimney fires, and having to haul the wood down to the kennel from the driveway, she said that's it! I watch as one man is pulling the big long hose across the lawn to the tank that is at the end of our kennel. Another man named Danny is talking to my mom. He is training the man with the hose. The last delivery that Danny made to our house was just before I came to live here.

So she's telling him about me. I hear her say. "You haven't seen my Rottweiler, his name is Quinn." And of course has to repeat the story of how my name was Chong, etc. And again I am so glad she changed it to Quinn. Even this propane guy laughs at the story and adds that Quinn is a much better name. That makes the pain go away for a short minute. I love hearing people say that Quinn is a great name. It makes me so very proud, that my mom felt that I deserved a finer name than one that was a joke.

"He's a nice looking dog and a big guy," Danny says, as he and my mom are standing there looking at me. My mom is really staring at me now, as Danny says that he thinks my leg looks swollen. My mom has noticed it at the same time, and gasps. "Oh, nooo, he had a Mast Cell tumor on his foot and had to have it and a toe removed, and now it looks like his lymph node is swollen bigger than ever."

She tells him that because it is in my lymph node, I'm getting chemo treatments to make me well again. They finish filling the tank, and my mom pays them. She waits while they pull the big truck out of our driveway, so she can close the gate behind them. She hurries back to the kennel to let us back out into the yard, before she runs into the house to call Mendocino Animal Hospital.

Jane answers the phone on the other end, asking my mom, "What's up?" My mom is so upset as she tells Jane about my leg. She says she has to get me in for a vet to look at it. "Bring him in and we will work him in between the other appointments."

My mom tells Jane that we will be there in a flash. She calls the other two dogs back to the kennel, telling them that they have to stay. She is now getting me into the car. She is trying to help me, but my leg hurts so bad, that I can't stop myself from letting out a yelp.

"Oh Quinn I'm so sorry buddy. I didn't mean to do that."

I plop down in the back. Even though my leg has horrible pain racing through it, I manage a smile, just because I'm in the car, and going for a ride.

We get to the door of the clinic and my mom opens it so we can go inside. I know the whole routine by heart now, so I automatically go to the pad on the floor, and stand on the scale to be weighed. I am holding my weight at 84lbs. I haven't eaten for over a day now, But I'll start to gain after the chemo treatments are all done. We go over to the end of the double row of chairs where my mom always sits. Erin asks, "What's up?"

My mom points to my back leg, which is now three times the size of my other one. I don't want to lie down, because it hurts to get back up. My mom goes over to the desk and asks Jane who will be my vet. Jane tells her that Dr. Bennett will look at me. After the bad experience with the new vet that treated Mae, my mom doesn't want any part of someone new looking at me. She just would rather wait. Jane says that she understands, and will go see what she can do. She comes back out to the desk and tells my mom that Dr. LaRue can see me.

"Thank you, I have nothing against Dr. Bennett. I don't know her, and just feel better with Dr. LaRue."

"That's fine, we understand what you're going through and you have to feel comfortable."

Again my mom thanks Jane for her help, and goes back to sit down. One of the nurses named Michele opens the door and motions for my mom to bring me into the exam room. She looks at my leg, and tells my mom that Dr. LaRue will be in shortly. Not a minute goes by and Dr. LaRue comes in. She greets my mom, asking her what's wrong. My mom shows her my leg. She looks at my chart and reads what Dr. Sara has written down. In my folder is all the information about me since my first visit.

Dr. LaRue looks me over, and has Michele draw blood, so she can see what's going on with me. I don't think my mom even noticed what a big boy I was, letting Michele stick the needle in my leg. Dr. LaRue looks me over before she sits on the stool and starts writing down the meds she wants me to take. It's back to all of the ones in the beginning, including the Prednisone, the one that makes me pee out of control. My mom looks so worried; she is trying to think while all of this information is coming at her, racing through her brain.

"Oh, this is not good at all, in two more days I have to give him four chemo pills on top of all this!?"

She is feeling like she is doing me more harm than good. Dr. LaRue sees the look on my moms face, and quietly says, "You know. All we're doing now is buying time."

My mom looks back at her and says. "Yeah…. and thank you for saying that, because I think we just ran out of time."

It hurts but I get up and follow my mom out to the lobby, and then to the car. On the way home, as I lay in back, I notice that my mom is crying softly to herself. She doesn't want me to see her do that, but she can't help it. I have a feeling that she knows something I don't. All the while I'm wondering why Dr. Sara didn't see me today. I don't realize that she is still in the hospital. People take a lot longer to get well after surgery than dogs do. I'm thinking, every time I went in for surgery, I got to go home that afternoon, only staying over night because my mom couldn't watch me the night of Ashley's graduation. And the time after surgery, and my foot was bloody.

We get home and my mom gets the gate and in we go. She goes and lets Ernie and Rosey out of the kennel. They come racing up to me, asking me about my leg. I don't want to talk right now, my leg is hurting me so bad. They understand and let me go in the house. I head straight for my bed.I can't lie down like I normally do. My leg is so swollen that it won't even bend. So I have to bend my other legs down slowly, until I'm about 2 inches from my blanket, and as I'm leaning to the right, I drop to the floor. I can't lay on my left side. My mom is bringing me something to eat. It smells so good. But no way am I going to eat. She helps me up to go outside, while she fixes my bed. This lady is so tuned into her dogs. She knows just how I like my blanket pushed, like dog beds that have a bolster on one side. She takes the top layer of my blanket and bunches it up all on one side for me. It would be to hard for me to do this, because it is hard to stand on my leg now. It is so swollen that I'm beginning to get creases in my skin like a Shar-pei.

My mom lets me back in the door, and I go straight over to my bed. Slowly lowering myself down to the blanket. The stove is going because tonight it's very cold out. There's still six more weeks to go before winter, but at night it feels like it's already come. Except in the daytime it has been warm and mild, in the middle 70's and hardly any wind. One of those fall days, where it is wonderful lying on the deck, soaking up the sun. On days like that it will also be very still and not very many noises, and I feel like I'm laying in Mother Natures arms, and she is holding me so very close, where nothing can harm me. My mom told me just the other day, when we were having one of our one-on-one talks. I shake her hand and she talks to me. It had been a day just like the one I mentioned, except she said that it really was Mother Nature's way of telling people that winter was just around the corner. That you should be prepared and ready. And if you didn't have your firewood by now, you were going to be in trouble. Meaning the wood you most likely get now would be green.

Every hour or so, my mom comes down to see how I'm doing. She again puts my leash on and gently pulls me up until I'm standing. Then leads me to the door and outside. When I come back in, I head right for my bed and drop, facing the closet wall. My mom comes over to me and grabs one side of my bed with both hands and pulls it until it is turned around, so I'm now facing toward the door. This way, she can pull me up and out the next time I have to go outside.

It's time for everyone to settle down for the night, and my mom comes to sit down on the stair by my bed. She is talking to me, while she is stroking my fur, in a caressing motion of her hand and is scratching me behind my ears. Petting me on my head, she tells me how lucky she was to have had me in her life. She whispers to me. "Hey buddy, remember when I said to you,…"

She pauses, as I answer her with a soft, "Grrrr".

"As long as your tail is wagging and you have a smile on your face."

She pauses again and I give out a soft low, "Grrrr."

"I'll keep on doing everything I can to help you get well."

As she stops stroking my fur, I answer her with another grrrr. Looking at me with tears swelling up in her eyes, she says,

"You're not growling at me, your talking Rottie-talk.

She is sitting on the stairs and leaning on the carpet by my bed. My back is towards her, but I can turn my head and see her just fine. She puts her head down on her arm, and is so sad. I look at her and feel her sadness. If I were a human I would give her a big hug. I want her to know that I love her and understand what she is doing for me. So I gently put my head right on top of hers, giving her a hug. This is the only way I feel I can let her know that this struggle is over for me.

My last ride to the vet's.

CHAPTER 20

My Last Journey

I have stopped wagging my tail. It's not that I'm not happy, but I know I can't do anything anymore because of the pain. It is now constant, and I know that it's time for me to go on to another place. I will miss my Dr. Sara, and my auntie Terry. And all the friends that I made at the animal hospital. In my whole lifetime, I never had that many human friends all at the same time. And my animal friends that turned out to be my buddies will be missed. I will also miss peeking through the fence at Dakota. I sure hope Ernie doesn't continue to tease him, because someday that fence might fall down, and then Ernie will be in a world of hurt. It could very well be from the fence falling on him, and not Dakota. My friend Rosey will watch out for my mom, continuing to run up the driveway in the morning to grab the paper and bring it back. She loves doing that. She told me that she would make sure my mom was safe, and I didn't have to worry. She has been the best mom I could ever have hoped for. I have been a very lucky boy living with this family.

I've been thinking about my Dr. Sara, and hope her knee will soon be good and not give her any more discomfort. She didn't give up on me, when I was being a grumbling tough guy at the clinic. I could tell that she loved me very much, in the way her face would light up when she saw me. And I would wiggle my tail really fast back and forth when I saw her, to let her know that I knew I was very special to her. So, I have decided that now is the best time for me to go, while she is still in the hospital. I don't want Dr. Sara to have to be the one to send me on my way. After all she did trying to make me well, it wouldn't be right. I have given my mom the okay for her to make the arrangements, and let her know that this is my decision.

It is now Thursday, and I haven't eaten since Monday morning. My mom has just brought me down some scrambled eggs with cheese mixed in. It smells delicious, but I can't eat it. She helps pull me up to go outside. Oh, how my leg hurts. It looks like the size of a leg of lamb. It is so swollen and I can't put any weight on it. I hobble to the door and limp out to the lawn, and back inside to my blanket. This is where I want to stay for the rest of the day. Ernie and Rosey are letting me be. We have already said our good-byes. And they know that I don't feel like talking to them anymore. Lillie came to me in the night, and surprised me by curling up next to me, and falling asleep for part of the night. She told me that I renewed her trust in big dogs. And that she thought that I was pretty special. I told her thank you, but remember all dogs aren't as sensitive and trusting as I am, and to keep her guard up. She thanked me, and at the same time put her paw up to the side of my head in what I would say was a gentle pat, letting me know that she truly cared for me. And then in a split second, she was up on the dresser looking out the window, as the break of dawn began. She turned her head towards me, and in her cat-like way, she narrowed her eyes saying.

"May your journey be fast, my brother, soon you will be meeting others in our family who have passed, and they will look out for you."

She is a very wise cat for being only four years old. I feel so lucky that I was able to befriend a cat like her. She helped round out my life, with her playful jesters aimed at me. Even though she never let me put her head in my mouth like Rosey did, we had formed a trusting relationship. It is 9 am, and I hear my mom making the phone call to the vets office.

"Yes." She says into the phone, as she is talking to Jane. "We will be there at noon, thank you."

She slowly hangs up the phone. I don't hear her moving around, so I know she is sitting on the stairs. A long time seems to pass until she comes down stairs. She sits beside me, and as she is softly talking to me, gives me a big wonderful hug.

"Oh, Quinn I wish it could have turned out differently, and that you could have been here at least one more year. We didn't get to do all the things good dogs like you get to do." She says to me with tears in her eyes. "You would've been so good at the obedience trials."

I look at her with sad eyes, only because it makes me sad to see her like this. It hurts me that I have to leave, knowing in the short time I was here, she loved me like nobody has ever loved me. The days that I spent here, whether painful or not, were the best days of my life. And with every bit of strength I have left in me, I give her one last wiggle of my tail. letting her know that what is about to happen is okay with me. And with the wiggle, I'm telling her that I love her very much. She stands and goes up stairs, telling me that she will be right back.

My mom has gone outside with Ernie and Rosey, doing something that must be really special. Because Ernie is jumping all around, as I hear him telling her to hurry up, he can't wait. I don't have a clue to what she is doing, but will find out as soon as she comes back in the house. She is now coming back down the stairs to where I'm laying. She says to me, "I had to give them their Frosty Paws outside, before I brought you yours."

She had put mine in the microwave oven just for a couple of seconds, to soften it up for me. It would have been too frozen for me to lick. She sits down next to me and takes two of her fingers and scoops out just a little bit for me to taste. Oh, thank you for doing this, I think as I slowly lick her fingers. Even though I haven't eaten since Monday, I have no trouble licking this deliciously wonderful doggie ice cream. She scoops out another gob of the soft yummy treat. She repeats the scooping until it is all gone. That was the finest last meal anyone could ask for.

Soon my mom's friend, Derek, shows up. He is going to come with us. He has been one of my good friends since the day I came to live here. He has known my mom's other Rottweilers, and knows how much she cares for them. He also loves Ernie and Rosey. He puts them in the kennel, and helps my mom get me up the stairs and out the door to the car, where he gently lifts me into the back. As my mom is backing out of the gate, I get a grin on my face. Oh boy I get to go for a car ride, how cool is that? I'm smiling now. They can't see that I'm also wiggling my tail just for a second or two. Derek gets into the car and is holding up something in front of him and my mom. It's his cell phone, with a camera. Who would have thought, those two things all wrapped up in one. It's a good thing that he has his cell phone with him, because the way things are going to happen are so different than they were when she brought her other dogs in for this. If she had any idea what was going to happen, she would certainly want her camera with her. He clicks off a couple of pictures of me in the back, smiling for the camera. I'm such a ham when it comes to having my picture taken. In all the pictures my mom has, I am smiling at whoever is taking them. We are off to the vets, as I lie here looking out at the trees slowly passing by. My mom isn't driving very fast; I think she is trying to make our last ride together special. She is definitely not in a hurry. She knows that we have to be there at noon, so she has left a little bit earlier so she can do just what she is doing.

The parking lot has only two cars in it. It's very unusual for this lot to be empty. But there's a reason for this. My mom drives in looking for a spot to park. Well, we certainly have plenty of choices to pick from, I am laughing to myself about what is going on, and wondering what my crazy mom is thinking. When we would come here for my appointments, we always got a parking place and the lot would be full. What, oh what is she doing? The car is pulling to the side of the clinic. She has done this because it's 74 degrees outside today. And it would be too hot, because It's lunchtime and the sun is straight up, with no shade at all. It is a fine Fall day, without a breeze anywhere.

My Mom gets out, and goes inside to let them know that we are here. Derek is out of the car and opens the hatchback up. The seats in the back are folded down as always, so I can stretch out and be comfortable. As soon as the back opens up, I can see the clump of Redwood trees, the ones where I always left a message for the next dog that came along. They are special to me, because they were part of my visit to see my Dr. Sara. I'm thinking about Dr. Sara as I'm looking at the trees, the clinic where all my friends and Dr. Sara were. This was a big part of the change that happened to me nine short months ago.

My mom enters the lobby, where nurse Kathy is waiting for her. She wants to come out and check out the situation. My mom greets her and starts for the door, with nurse Kathy following. Halfway to the door my mom stops and turns around. Tina is standing on the other side of the desk, as Erin, Susan, Jane and Michelle are sitting silently staring at my mom and what is about to take place. "Would you ladies like to come out and say good-bye to Quinn?" she asks them.

They jump up, taking turns coming out to see me. I hear voices getting louder as I begin to see some of my friends walking towards the car, following my mom. Jane tells my mom that she will be back, because someone has to cover the phones. Giving my friends time to come outside. It makes me happy when I see them coming to say farewell to me. Each one takes her turn and gives me a hug and says what a great guy I am, and that they love me very much. They never said hi to me without digging into the treat jar. Boy I was a lucky guy to have known all of them. Now, who would of thought going to the vets would turn out to be my favorite thing. I can't forget the yummy treats I always got there. You've got to know that there isn't another dog around that loves cookies and treats more than me. Well maybe my pal Ernie has me beat, just because he's older than me. And the rides here were always fun. Ridin in the car with my mom was nothing but the best.

Kathy goes to tell Dr. Bennett that we are ready. This is the new vet that my mom didn't want to have examine me. She had nothing against her, but just that she was new. She comes out to meet my mom.

She introduces herself, "Hi it's nice to meet you, my name is Jenn."

I can tell by the way my mom is looking and talking to her, that she likes her right off. And isn't uncomfortable about her anymore with the undertaking that she is about to endure shortly.

One by one the girls from the front desk have come back, taking turns, and giving me more hugs and pets on my head, again talking softly to me. Each one tells me they will miss me. I know they will certainly miss my big smily face, and wiggly tail. There are tears in all of their eyes, as they say their good-byes to me. There is enough room in the back with the hatch up, so that I can stand. I manage to pull myself up, as Tina comes over to see me. She is terribly upset, and I feel the love that she has for me. Jane comes back out as Erin goes back in to cover the front desk. I miss saying good-bye to Dr. Sara and my nurse auntie Terry, but I didn't want them to have to go through the pain my mom is experiencing right now. It is like when I was going to come live with my new family; I heard the girl say to my papa that it was for the best. I too felt that this was the right time and for the best. Also, I would hope that Dr. Sara would understand, and forgive me for not waiting for her to get well enough to be here; but it was time for me to go. I lay back down so Dr. Jenn can give me a shot to relax me. I feel a little fuzzy and warm feeling rush through me, at the same time I hear more voices next to the car as Denise comes up and gives my mom a hug and then turns to me, telling me good-bye. Next is my friend, Danny, who turned out to be one of my best buddies. Each one comes up to my mom and hugs her. It makes me feel very proud that she is my mom, that she was smart enough to know I deserved a better name than Chong. That guy was a dog who lived in a different world. When the lady changed my name, my life changed, and she also became my mom. This is why I mentioned earlier about my mom wanting her camera. Neither she nor I had any idea all of my friends would come out to the car to say their farewells to me. And had it been full of cars, nobody would have been able to say good-bye. So this is why I said everything is for a reason.

Dr. Jenn is back out to see how I'm doing. She quietly leans over to Kathy and says something that I can't hear. She has to give me another shot. I feel really weird and it scars me so, I jolt as I try to get up. But Kathy and my mom push me firmly back down with their hands, at the same time telling me that it's okay. They reassure me that everything is fine. That helps calm me some, and I relax a little bit more as the shot Dr. Jenn gave me is starting to work some now. She leaves for a minute, and my friends from the big room are turning and going back to take care of the pets that are inside. Just a hand full from the front desk are here, giving my mom support.

All of a sudden a big wind starts to come up, and is blowing hard enough that Derek has to grab the hatch-back from crashing down. Dr. Jenn is just returning to my car and mentions the wind coming up and it being a little chilly.

I hear my mom say,. "He's gonna need a good gust of wind to get him up and out, and on his way."

Dr. Jenn says something again to Kathy, who is looking at my mom. With tears in her eyes, she nods her head for Dr. Jenn to go ahead and do what has to be done. Nurse Kathy has a hold of my front leg, gently pulling it forward. She is going to stick a needle in my leg, and I don't even care. In a flash my mind goes back to when I first came to this clinic to be treated. Always giving them grumbled growls, and making things hard, when they were just trying to help me get well. That is when I feel the prick of the needle as it breaks through my skin. At the same time the noises around me start to fade away to silence, there is the force of a tornado like wind and in a flash I am up and out of my earthly body. I can't believe what I'm feeling! My leg or the other parts of me that were so painful are gone. It's almost like I have wings, as I am now hovering above my mom, who is hugging Dr. Jenn and the rest of my friends that are still there.

This is awesome to say the least. I don't hear anything, but for some reason I am aware that I have a short time before my journey is completed and I will be gone. This is so cool as I get to follow my mom's car carrying my earthly body back home to be buried in my favorite part of the yard. The car pulls slowly into the driveway, and Derek gets out to open the gate. I see the car disappear as it goes under the roof of the carport. Now I see my mom take Ernie and Rosey out to the back yard as Derek is carrying me to my resting place. This instant, (which is just a split second in time) is over and BAM with a full force of whatever.........I'm at The Rainbow Bridge. I normally would shake myself off, after something like that happened. But I don't have to do that here. I look around and see, off in the distance, some dogs that look just like me. They come over to meet me, welcoming me home. My journey is now over, as it was a quick and swift one. And so now I feel the time is right for me to say farewell to my special friend, Dr. Sara.

The next day I guide my mom over to the computer, as she is in a total fog and probably in shock. I am worried about what Dr. Sara will be thinking when she opens her email and sees the subject line saying: HELLO FROM THE RAINBOW BRIDGE

Hey....Dr. Sara, it's me, Quinn. I was really sick, and my leg swelled up, so it was hard to get up. I didn't want to eat anything that my mom offered me. I hadn't eaten since Monday. Finally my mom brought me a frosty paws ice cream for dogs. And I started licking it off her fingers. Boy was THAT good. I then went for a ride to MAH. Mom parked in the shade of the driveway, next to the big Redwood trees. She opened the back up, and wow I could lay there, and look all around. Next thing I see are my friends. The girls from the front desk. They came out one and two at a time. They wanted to say good-by to me. Then Denise, and Tina, and Hillary, and that guy with the hair on his face, Danny (I really got to like him) came out and said, "Good-by" That nice lady, Kathy brought Dr. Jenn out to meet me. She gave me a shot. It did something to me. But my mom & Kathy petted me and told me it was ok. Then you know what? That Dr. Jenn, gave me a shot that whizzed me up & out. BAM....here I am at the Rainbow Bridge. I looked around and there were some big dogs that looked just like me. They came over to greet me. And you know what? They said that they had the same mom that I had. I've been hanging out with the male dog, and he is showing me around. I feel so good now. I don't hurt anymore. I wanted to thank you for all the love and care you gave me; trying to make me well. I told my mom, please don't be sad, and stop crying. I told my new friends, that I miss my mom. And you know what? They told me that some day, I'll even be able to see her again. Isn't that cool?

Well, Dr. Sara, I gotta go now, cause the other dogs want to show me how to play hide and I go and find them. How much fun is that? Wow!!

Love, from your favorite Rottweiler, Quinn

EPILOGUE

Hi, I'm Quinn's mom, and because he is no longer with me I have to finish this part of his story. I must clarify something before I go on. Out of eight Rottweilers that I have had over the last 24 years, five had cancer. Quinn was the first to go through chemo, as I had done a year and half earlier, fighting Breast cancer. Dr. Rice and I were so hoping that he would survive this evil monster; and be able to enjoy a couple more years of the fun he was having living with the other two dogs and the cat. Yes, I was in a shocked state of mind, when for some reason or other, I got up and went to the computer, as if being lead there. I wasn't planning on doing anything but sit out in the yard and reminisce about the joy and fun Quinn brought into my life. While later on I would try to get a hold of Sara and tell her what and why it happened when it did. Quinn needed me to push the keys for him, so he could say good-bye to his favorite veterinarian, Dr. Sara. Without rereading it, I really can not tell exactly how the contents of his letter were written. Mainly because they were his words and not mine.

The next day I went online to check my email, and I saw in the subject line of in coming emails one from: Sara Rice. It said, Dear Quinn. I sat and just stared at it, longer than I normally do when I'm opening my emails. I opened it and slowly started to read the words that were there in front of me. This was something that was beyond anything I could imagine. Sara surely was not expecting or prepared to get Quinn's letter. In addition, I never thought there would be an answer back. As I read the words, it became very clear to me that there was a bond between the two of them like no other. From the trust that was built, to the lessons that were learned, this turned into a story that had to be shared. One could tell that the words that Sara wrote to Quinn and Jenn were from her heart. And what a huge heart it is.

My dearest Quinn--I was in no way ready to get your news of yesterday and so sad just doesn't even begin to describe how I felt...But in reading your words, I realized that you felt so much better now and that you weren't worried any more and that you had found new friends and maybe even some family---is that right? I always worried about big black dogs before I met you, but you and I figured out something together--that I could trust a big black dog and that you could trust me..so that was worth a whole bunch and I thank you for that.

I had surgery this week, I know that I told you and I think your mom did too and I have been in a lot of really terrible pain. The thing is that this pain will gradually get less and less and then I'll be pretty okay. Sounds like your pain was getting worse and worse and your pain wasn't going to get better. Maybe before this pain that I have, I couldn't quite understand how awful it is, but now that I have and am living that, I know that I wouldn't want you to live that way..ya know what I mean? I was so happy the first night in the hospital, because the only thing cheery thing in my room was your bouquet and I brought them home and they still look wonderful. I miss you terribly, Quinn, you have been a wonderful friend to me and your mom and all those MAH folks...we are all better people for having known you.

Dr. Jenn is wonderful and I am so glad that you did get to meet her--she's a gentle and loving soul...as are you. Keep an eye out for some little black and white dogs, with no tails and pointy ears--if you meet mr T--let him know that you and I were special friends. Miss you so much, XXXS

You have read in the story about how I didn't want any new veterinarians treating my boy. I want to say that Dr. Bennett is as wonderful as Dr. Rice said she is. I was curious as to when she had graduated. She told me that she had gone to the University of Wisconsin-Madison School of Veterinary Medicine. Later I found out that this fine young woman graduated in June of this same year that this story took place, 2008. I felt after the way she handled this very painful experience, that I at anytime will be able to make an appointment with her. This was a lesson I learned and came away with; that I will not be afraid of the new/young ones anymore. Knowing that my pets will be in safe and good hands.

Dr. Rice forwarded an email to me that she had sent to Dr. Bennett, thanking her for Quinn, as she was still out from work, recuperating from her surgery. My email read: Fr: Thanks for Quinn, it said....This is the thank you that I sent to Jenn..S

Subject: Thanks for Quinn Dear Jenn--I have been meaning to send you this note of thanks since I learned of Quinn's passing. He sent me a beautiful note from the other side of the Rainbow Bridge where he said he had met a lot of big black dogs that looked like him and had maybe even met his mother!! So I knew that he had moved on, but he also said that he really liked you and was glad to have met you before he left. His mom, Maryly (one of those people who might say...oh, no the young/new ones please), absolutely adored you and was so warmed by the care that you gave to Quinn and to her.

I have known a LOT of Rottweilers in my practice years and generally like/respect/or fear them. Quinn came to me a growly, scared guy who had lived on a chain for 8 years. He was 'sort of' okay in the rooms, but a definite grumbler. Once his cancer developed, he and I had an epiphany together....Gina was placing a catheter, Danny was laying on him (very movable despite his drugs), he was muzzled and growling and I stood in front of him and repeated over and over, "you have got to trust me, you have got to trust me, you have got to trust me." Now this isn't something that is in my bag of tricks and I know I had never really been that specific and direct before, but everyone in the room saw it happen...his grumbling lessened and he relaxed and after that, he got his iv's usually with nothing more than an arm around his head. So I/we helped him trust people and he changed my opinion of Rotties. So he was a real special guy to me and although I had hoped he would survive my absence, I wasn't shocked by the news. I even wonder if he was waiting for me to go, to make it easier on me. If this all sounds too crazy chalk it up to pain and pain meds and awareness of pain in others...boy has this been an eye opener. What I want to say, Jenn, is that you did a terrific job with Quinn and his mom and you have been doing a terrific job for us at MAH and for all your patients and have set a wonderful example to the staff. I am so delighted that you have joined us….Hugs, Sara

CPSIA information can be obtained at www.ICGtesting.com
Printed in the USA
BVOW080002241012

303766BV00001B/3/P